MW00844169

METALWORK TECHNOLOGY AND PRACTICE STUDENT WORKBOOK

Ninth Edition

Victor E. Repp, Ed. D.
Professor Emeritus of Manufacturing Technology
College of Technology
Bowling Green State University
Bowling Green, Ohio

For use with the textbook *Metalwork Technology and Practice*

 **Glencoe McGraw-Hill**

New York, New York   Columbus, Ohio   Woodland Hills, California   Peoria, Illinois

Glencoe/McGraw-Hill

A Division of The McGraw-Hill Companies

Copyright © 1994, 1989, 1982, 1975, 1969, 1962, and 1956 by Glencoe/McGraw-Hill. All rights reserved. Except as permitted under the United States Copyright Act, no part of this publication may be reproduced or distributed in any form or by any means, or stored in a database or retrieval system, without prior written permission from the publisher.

Send all inquires to:
Glencoe/McGraw-Hill
3008 W. Willow Knolls Drive
Peoria, IL   61614-1083

ISBN 0-02-676486-5 (Student Workbook)
ISBN 0-02-676484-9 (Text)
ISBN 0-02-676485-7 (Instructor's Resource Guide)

Printed in the United States of America

8 9 10 11 12 13 14 069 07

Introduction

This workbook is intended for use with the textbook **Metalwork Technology and Practice.** The organization of the workbook matches that of the text, part by part and unit by unit. The questions and exercises are largely short-answer, multiple-choice, or matching types. There are also several calculation and drawing exercises. Each question or exercise is designed to test a key point or idea presented in the corresponding unit in the textbook, and each workbook unit may serve as a review of the corresponding text material.

Instructors may use the workbook in several ways. Selected questions or parts of units may be used for short quizzes. Whole units may be assigned in connection with reading assignments in the text. The exercises or questions may reveal specific student difficulties or point out topics that, for one reason or another, are not well understood. Instructors will also find the workbook helpful in developing examinations on units or parts in the text. Lastly, advanced students may be challenged by extra reading in the text and related unit assignments in the workbook.

Contents

Name *Justin Stilwell*

Score _____

UNIT 1
Careers in Metalworking

1-12. Multiple Choice. Write the letter of the correct response to each statement or question in the space at the left.

B   1. A book published by the U.S. Department of Labor that provides current information about all types of careers is the
   A. Dictionary of Occupational Titles   C. Career Quarterly
   B. Occupational Outlook Handbook   D. Career Outlook Review

A   2. There are over 20,000 occupational titles described in the U.S. Department of Labor book called the
   A. Dictionary of Occupational Titles   C. Career Quarterly Handbook
   B. Occupational Outlook Handbook   D. Annual Survey of Occupational Titles

C   3. The length of time usually required to train an engineer or a machinist is
   A. 2 years   C. 4 years
   B. 3 years   D. 5 years

A   4. Workers in occupations that require little or no training are classified as
   A. unskilled   C. skilled
   B. semi-skilled   D. technicians

C   5. An example of a semi-skilled occupation would be a(n)
   A. engineer   C. machine tool operator
   B. floor sweeper   D. technologist

D   6. An example of a skilled occupation is
   A. technician   C. engineer
   B. technologist   D. tradesperson (such as machinist)

D   7. A person learning a trade in a systematic way under a master of the trade or under the direction of a company is called a(n)
   A. beginner   C. trainee
   B. learner   D. apprentice

A   8. Becoming a skilled tradesperson without the benefit of a formal educational program is called
   A. the pickup method   C. an apprenticeship
   B. on-the-job training   D. an internship

(Continued on next page)

_C_   9. Workers whose occupations require two years of technical education beyond high school are called
    A. engineers   C. technicians
    B. technologists   D. skilled workers

_C_   10. Which occupational classification requires four years of college and prepares industrial workers for either technical or middle-management positions?
    A. journeyman   C. technologist
    B. technician   D. engineer

_B_   11. The occupational classification requiring the highest level of education in mathematics, physics, and chemistry is
    A. technician   C. technologist
    B. engineer   D. skilled tradesperson

_D_   12. The kind of engineer who organizes people, materials, and machines for mass production in an industrial plant is the
    A. tool engineer   C. industrial engineer
    B. manufacturing engineer   D. all of the above

Name _Justin Stilwell_

Score _____

UNIT 2
Introducing Metals

1-16. Multiple Choice. Write the letter of the correct response to each statement or question in the space at the left.

___C___ 1. Characteristics of metals when they are **not** being acted upon by outside forces are called
A. chemical qualities   C. physical properties
B. attributes   D. traits

___C___ 2. Characteristics of the chemical composition of metals are called
A. mechanical properties   C. chemical properties
B. physical properties   D. molecular properties

___A___ 3. Characteristics that describe how metals behave when outside forces are applied are called
A. mechanical properties   C. chemical properties
B. physical properties   D. molecular properties

___A___ 4. What property of metal refers to its ability to resist penetration?
A. hardness   C. elasticity
B. toughness   D. elastic limit

___B___ 5. What property of metal refers to its ability to withstand shock without cracking?
A. hardness   C. strength
B. toughness   D. elasticity

___D___ 6. The property that causes metal to break with little or no bending is
A. hardness   C. fatigue
B. toughness   D. brittleness

___C___ 7. The property of metal that refers to its resistance to being pulled apart is
A. ductility   C. tensile strength
B. toughness   D. compressive strength

___A___ 8. Metals high in weldability are usually high in
A. fusibility   C. malleability
B. ductility   D. meltability

___D___ 9. The property that causes metal to fracture under a repeated load that is less than the tensile strength of the metal is called
A. elastic limit   C. toughness
B. brittleness   D. fatigue

(Continued on next page)

_B_   10. Ferrous metals are metals that contain
- A. copper
- B. iron
- C. aluminum
- D. zinc

_D_   11. A combination of two or more metals, one of which is intentionally added to the base metal, is called a(n)
- A. mixture
- B. compound
- C. blend
- D. alloy

_D_   12. Steels that can be hardened to make such items as files, drills, wrenches, and hammers are called
- A. alloy steels
- B. structural steels
- C. specialty steels
- D. tool steels

_C_   13. About how many different kinds of metals and metal alloys are now available?
- A. 1,000
- B. 10,000
- C. 20,000
- D. 30,000

_B_   14. About how many different kinds of aluminum alloys are available?
- A. 400
- B. 350
- C. 300
- D. 250

_C_   15. About how many kinds of copper alloys are available?
- A. 100
- B. 200
- C. 300
- D. 400

_B_   16. About how many different kinds of metals are used in a modern automobile?
- A. 50
- B. 100
- C. 150
- D. 200

Name ___Justin Stikwell___

Score _____

UNIT 3
Personal Safety in Metalworking

1-13. Short Answer. In the spaces provided below, write 13 things that the boy pictured needs to correct to be dressed safely for work.

1. ___Needs safety glasses___
2. ___Must tuck tie in___
3. ___Must roll up sleeves above elbow___
4. ___No torn pockets___
5. ___No wristwatch___
6. ___No gloves___
7. ___Must have a clean apron that fits close to body___
8. ___Must have apron that only hangs to knees___
9. ___Apron strings need to be tied around the back___
10. ___No rings___
11. ___No sweaters___
12. ___Must wear safety shoes___
13. ___Must have short hair or wear a small cap___

14-24. Multiple Choice. Write the letter of the correct response to each statement or question in the space at the left.

14. Clothing made of which kind of fabric is safest to work in?
    A. soft and smooth   C. hard and smooth
    B. soft and fuzzy   D. hard and ribbed

15. Next to safety shoes, what shoes offer good protection for metalworking?
    A. ordinary leather shoes C. open-toe sandals
    B. canvas shoes   D. any of the above

(Continued on next page)

_C_ 16. Long hair should be kept close to a worker's head with a
    A. headband   C. close-fitting cap
    B. loose-fitting cap   D. either A or C

_B_ 17. The safest way to remove sharp metal chips from machines is with
    A. the hands   C. a rag
    B. a brush   D. compressed air

_B_ 18. Before picking up a piece of metal you suspect is hot, check its temperature
    A. with a thermometer   C. by looking to see if it is red-hot
    B. by sprinkling a few drops of water   D. by touching it quickly with a wet
       on it   finger

_D_ 19. When is it safe to leave a machine while it is running?
    A. when no cutting is being done   C. when no one else is near the machine
    B. at the beginning of a long cut using   D. never
       power feed

_B_ 20. When lifting heavy objects from the floor, what part of the body should provide most
of the lifting power?
    A. arms   C. back
    B. legs   D. hands

_D_ 21. Sharp-edged tools
    A. are safer to use than dull tools   C. should be handed to another person
    B. should be carried sharp edge down   handle first
                                           D. all of the above

_D_ 22. If you injure yourself, even slightly, in the shop or laboratory, the first person you
should tell is
    A. your mother   C. the school nurse
    B. your doctor   D. your instructor

_D_ 23. What kinds of burns should be treated by a doctor?
    A. first-degree burns   C. third-degree burns
    B. second-degree burns   D. both B and C

_A_ 24. To prevent spontaneous combustion, what kind of container should be used for
storing oily rags or waste?
    A. a closed metal container   C. a wire mesh container
    B. an open-topped metal container   D. any of the above

Name ___Justin Stilwell___

Score _____

UNIT 4
Iron

1-11. Multiple Choice. Write the letter of the correct response to each statement or question in the space at the left.

_C_   1. In the United States, iron ore is found mostly in which three states?
A. Montana, Michigan, Minnesota   C. Alabama, Michigan, Minnesota
B. Minnesota, New York, Michigan   D. Virginia, New York, Alabama

_D_   2. A low-grade iron ore now widely used is
A. siderite   C. hematite
B. limonite   D. taconite

_B_   3. The furnace for converting iron ore into pig iron is the
A. Bessemer converter   C. open hearth furnace
B. blast furnace   D. basic oxygen furnace

_D_   4. The material used in the blast furnace that combines the ash and iron ore impurities to form slag is
A. coke   C. waste gas
B. hot air   D. limestone

_B_   5. The range of carbon content in cast iron is
A. 3 to 5 percent   C. 1.7 to 4.5 percent
B. 1.7 to 6 percent   D. 0.05 to 2 percent

_A_   6. Pig iron that is remelted and poured into a mold to make a useful product is called
A. cast iron   C. wrought iron
B. pig casting iron   D. white cast iron

_A_   7. What kind of iron is used for machine frames, water hydrants, large pipes, and machine parts in which strength is not very important?
A. gray cast iron   C. malleable iron
B. white cast iron   D. wrought iron

_B_   8. Which form of iron is so hard it can be machined only by grinding?
A. gray cast iron   C. ductile iron
B. white cast iron   D. malleable iron

_D_   9. Malleable iron is made from which form of iron?
A. pig iron   C. gray cast iron
B. wrought iron   D. white cast iron

(Continued on next page)

B　10. What two kinds of iron are used for making tough castings for automobiles and farm machinery?
　　A. wrought iron and malleable iron　　C. malleable iron and wrought iron
　　B. ductile iron and malleable iron　　D. wrought iron and gray cast iron

A　11. The kind of iron that has practically no carbon and that has been largely replaced with hot-rolled low-carbon steel is
　　A. wrought iron　　C. malleable iron
　　B. ductile iron　　D. gray cast iron

12-16. Matching. Match the letters from the blast furnace illustration to the part names given below. Write the correct letters in the blanks at the left.

D　12. Slag ladle

C　13. Skip car

A　14. Stove

B　15. Blast furnace

E　16. Pig iron ladle

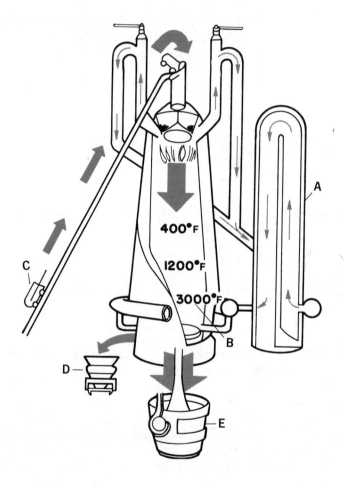

Name _Justin Stilwell_

Score _____

UNIT 5
Steelmaking

1-12. Multiple Choice. Write the letter of the correct response to each statement or question in the space at the left.

_A_ 1. The percentage of carbon in steel ranges from
A. 0.05 to 1.7 percent   C. 2 to 4.5 percent
B. 1.7 to 6 percent   D. 0.05 to 6 percent

_B_ 2. The steelmaking process that blows pure oxygen through pig iron to burn off excess carbon and impurities is the
A. electric process   C. open-hearth process
B. basic oxygen process   D. blast process

_A_ 3. The most important advantage of the open-hearth steel-making process is that it allows
A. heavy iron and steel scrap to be used   C. steel to be made in very large batches
B. short production time   D. close control of the chemical analysis of the steel

_B_ 4. The furnace used for making high-carbon steel, stainless steel, and other steel alloys with high melting points is the
A. electric induction furnace   C. basic oxygen furnace
B. electric arc furnace   D. open-hearth furnace

_C_ 5. Most steel made in the United States is now made by which process?
A. open-hearth   C. basic oxygen
B. electric arc   D. Bessemer

_C_ 6. A high-technology tool now being used in the production of sheet steel for measurement, inspection, alignment, and improvement of magnetic properties is the
A. robot   C. laser
B. nuclear gage   D. electron beam

_D_ 7. Converting liquid steel directly into slabs, blooms, or billets is called
A. rolling   C. ingot casting
B. direct reduction D. continuous casting

_C_ 8. Steel is made into sheets, plates, bars, and other shapes in machines called
A. rolling machines   C. rolling mills
B. presses   D. continuous casters

(Continued on next page)

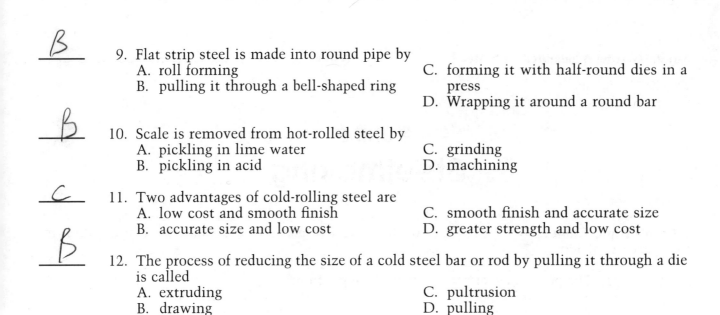

_B_ 9. Flat strip steel is made into round pipe by
           A. roll forming
           B. pulling it through a bell-shaped ring
           C. forming it with half-round dies in a press
           D. Wrapping it around a round bar

_B_ 10. Scale is removed from hot-rolled steel by
           A. pickling in lime water
           B. pickling in acid
           C. grinding
           D. machining

_C_ 11. Two advantages of cold-rolling steel are
           A. low cost and smooth finish
           B. accurate size and low cost
           C. smooth finish and accurate size
           D. greater strength and low cost

_B_ 12. The process of reducing the size of a cold steel bar or rod by pulling it through a die is called
           A. extruding
           B. drawing
           C. pultrusion
           D. pulling

Name *Justin Stilwell*

Score _____

UNIT 6
Kinds of Steel

1-19. Multiple Choice. Write the letter of the correct response to each statement or question in the space at the left.

_D_ 1. The two main kinds of steel are
A. low-carbon steels and high-carbon steels
B. plain carbon steels and high-speed steels
C. low-carbon steels and medium-carbon steels
D. plain carbon steels and alloy steels

_B_ 2. The carbon content of low-carbon steels ranges from
A. 0.005-0.03%
B. 0.05-0.30%
C. 0.50-3.0%
D. 5.0-30.0%

_B_ 3. The carbon content of medium-carbon steel ranges from
A. 0.05-0.30%
B. 0.30-0.60%
C. 0.60-1.50%
D. 3.0-6.0%

_B_ 4. The carbon content of high-carbon steel ranges from
A. 6.0-15.0%
B. 0.60-1.50%
C. 0.05-0.30%
D. 0.06-0.15%

_B_ 5. Because of the kind of products for which it is used, high-carbon steel is also called
A. high-speed steel
B. tool steel
C. all-purpose steel
D. free-machining carbon steel

_A_ 6. Round bars of high-carbon steel that have been ground and polished to accurate sizes are called
A. drill rod
B. tool steel rod
C. drill stock
D. dowel rod

_C_ 7. Steels that are specially made for easy machining are called
A. high-spccd steels
B. high-machining steels
C. free-machining steels
D. easy-machining steels

_D_ 8. Two materials added to steels to improve their machinability are
A. zinc and lead
B. sulfur and zinc
C. lead and sodium
D. lead and sulfur

_B_ 9. A new metal made by melting two or more metals together is called a(n)
A. mixture
B. alloy
C. compound
D. amalgam

(Continued on next page)

A

10. Which one of the following **is not** one of the three most important properties of steel that can be improved by alloying?
    A. strength through heat treatment
    B. hardenability
    C. corrosion resistance
    D. retention of hardness and strength at high temperatures

C

11. Which one of the following **is not** one of the three categories of alloy steels?
    A. alloy tool steels
    B. special alloy steels
    C. alloy machinery steels
    D. constructional alloy steels

B

12. The principle metal alloyed with steel to make stainless steel is
    A. nickel
    B. chromium
    C. copper
    D. cobalt

D

13. A metal used in the making of high-speed steel, cast alloys, and cemented carbide cutting tools is
    A. chromium
    B. nickel
    C. molybdenum
    D. cobalt

B

14. A metal alloyed with steel to improve its wear and shock resistance is
    A. tungsten
    B. manganese
    C. molybdenum
    D. chromium

C

15. Molybdenum is alloyed with steel to improve its
    A. corrosion resistance
    B. wear resistance
    C. strength and hardness
    D. machinability

B

16. A tough metal alloyed with steel to make cables, axles, and armor plate is
    A. chromium
    B. nickel
    C. manganese
    D. vanadium

B

17. Of all metals, the one with the highest melting point is
    A. vanadium
    B. tungsten
    C. manganese
    D. nickel

D

18. A metal alloyed with steel to give it a fine grain and improve its toughness and strength is
    A. nickel
    B. chromium
    C. tungsten
    D. vanadium

B

19. High-speed steel cutting tools keep their hardness up to a temperature of about
    A. 400° F [204° C]
    B. 1100° F [593° C]
    C. 1500° F [816° C]
    D. 1700° F [927° C]

Name _____

Score _____

UNIT 7
Nonferrous Metals and Their Alloys

1-29. Multiple Choice. Write the letter of the correct response to each statement or question in the space at the left.

_____   1. Aluminum melts at a temperature of about
      A. 600° F [316° C]   C. 1800° F [982° C]
      B. 1200° F [649° C]   D. 2400° F [1316° C]

_____   2. The ore from which aluminum is made is
      A. alumina   C. taconite
      B. bauxite   D. cryolite

_____   3. The alloy number of pure aluminum is
      A. 2024   C. 7075
      B. 6061   D. 1100

_____   4. Work-hardened aluminum can be softened by heating and slow cooling. How hot should it be heated?
      A. 350° F [177° C]   C. 850° F [454° C]
      B. 650° F [343° C]   D. 1100° F [593° C]

_____   5. The strongest of the following aluminum alloys is
      A. 7075   C. 2024
      B. 6061   D. 1100

_____   6. Babbitt is an alloy made of lead, copper, antimony, and
      A. zinc   C. tin
      B. aluminum   D. magnesium

_____   7. Babbitt is used mostly for
      A. protective coatings   C. bearings
      B. die castings   D. costume jewelry

_____   8. Why must special care be taken when machining beryllium?
      A. Its dust is toxic.   C. It wears tools out quickly.
      B. It burns easily.   D. It breaks easily.

_____   9. The cast alloys are a special group of alloys used mainly for making
      A. cutting tools   C. tough castings
      B. cutting tool holders   D. springs

(Continued on next page)

_____ 10. The oldest metal known to man is
- A. iron
- B. aluminum
- C. bronze
- D. copper

_____ 11. Copper can be made very tough by alloying it with
- A. zinc
- B. tin
- C. beryllium
- D. nickel

_____ 12. Work-hardened copper can be softened by heating it to a dull red color and quenching it
- A. in still air
- B. with compressed air
- C. in water
- D. in oil

_____ 13. German silver is a copper alloy that contains how much copper?
- A. 20%
- B. 30%
- C. 40%
- D. 50%

_____ 14. Brass is chiefly an alloy of copper and
- A. zinc
- B. tin
- C. lead
- D. nickel

_____ 15. Bronze is chiefly an alloy of copper and
- A. lead
- B. tin
- C. zinc
- D. nickel

_____ 16. A precious metal that can be hammered into sheets thinner than tissue paper is
- A. aluminum
- B. gold
- C. silver
- D. platinum

_____ 17. Pure gold is how many karats?
- A. 14
- B. 18
- C. 24
- D. 28

_____ 18. White gold is an alloy of gold and
- A. aluminum
- B. platinum
- C. silver
- D. nickel

_____ 19. A soft, heavy, widely-used metal that is also poisonous is
- A. lead
- B. tin
- C. zinc
- D. copper

_____ 20. Magnesium is a metal valued chiefly for its
- A. high strength
- B. low melting point
- C. ductility
- D. light weight

_____ 21. Special care must be taken when machining magnesium because
- A. it burns easily
- B. it breaks easily
- C. its dust is a health hazard
- D. it wears out tools quickly

_____ 22. Space-age alloys such as Inconel® and Hastelloy® contain a high percentage of what metal?
- A. titanium
- B. nickel
- C. chromium
- D. copper

_____ 23. A tin alloy used for tableware and ornamental work is
        A. babbitt   C. muntz metal
        B. pewter   D. monel metal

_____ 24. Of the following, the best conductor of electricity is
        A. copper   C. silver
        B. gold   D. aluminum

_____ 25. Sterling silver is an alloy of silver and
        A. gold   C. copper
        B. nickel   D. tin

_____ 26. By weight, what percentage of a tin can is made of tin?
        A. 100%   C. 10%
        B. 50%   D. less than 1%

_____ 27. A strong, light-weight, heat-resistant metal used for supersonic aircraft parts is
        A. magnesium   C. tungsten
        B. tantalum   D. titanium

_____ 28. Combining this metal with carbon and cobalt produces an extremely hard metal widely used for cutting tools.
        A. chromium   C. tungsten
        B. manganese   D. vanadium

_____ 29. Galvanizing protects iron and steel from rusting by coating it with a layer of
        A. lead   C. tin
        B. zinc   D. copper

Name _____

Score _____

UNIT 8
Metal Designation and Identification

1-13. Multiple Choice. Write the letter of the correct response to each statement or question in the space at the left.

_____ 1. The first digit of the SAE/AISI steel numbering system indicates
A. the percentage of alloying metal   C. the basic kind of steel
B. the percentage of carbon   D. whether the metal is ferrous or non-ferrous

_____ 2. The second digit of the SAE/AISI steel numbering system is often used to indicate
A. the percentage of alloying metal   C. the basic kind of steel
B. the percentage of carbon   D. a variation of the basic kind of steel

_____ 3. The last two or three digits of an SAE/AISI steel number are used to indicate
A. the percentage of carbon   C. the basic kind of steel
B. the percentage of alloying metal   D. a variation of the basic kind of steel

_____ 4. A steel numbered 1045 has how much carbon in it?
A. 45%   C. 0.45%
B. 4.5%   D. 0.045%

_____ 5. What is the main alloying element in a steel numbered 4130?
A. carbon   C. tungsten
B. chromium   D. molybdenum

_____ 6. By what system are commonly used tool and die steels identified?
A. the standard SAE/AISI system   C. a special system using a letter followed by one or more numbers
B. a special system for each steel manufacturer   D. a special name for each steel

_____ 7. What does the first digit of the wrought aluminum alloy numbering system indicate?
A. the percentage of alloying element   C. the percentage of carbon
B. the name of the main alloying element   D. the percentage of impurities

_____ 8. What is the main alloying element in an aluminum numbered 2011?
A. lead   C. aluminum
B. zinc   D. copper

(Continued on next page)

9. The temper designation included with the wrought aluminum alloy number indicates the
   A. degree of hardness as compared to the range of hardness possible for that alloy
   B. relative hardness as compared to all wrought aluminum alloys
   C. machinability of the alloy
   D. weldability of the alloy

10. What is the name of the new numbering system being adopted for all metals?
    A. The Universal Numbering System
    B. The American Standard Numbering System
    C. The National Standard Numbering System
    D. The Unified Numbering System

11. The color painted on the ends of steel bars
    A. is for rust protection
    B. tells what kind of steel it is
    C. tells what wholesaler supplied the metal
    D. tells what steel mill made the metal

12. When you cut a piece of steel from a bar, start
    A. from the painted end
    B. from the unpainted end
    C. with a spark test
    D. from the middle

13. In the spark-testing of steels, what does a high volume of sparks mean?
    A. high alloy content
    B. high carbon content
    C. low alloy content
    D. low carbon content

Name _____

Score _____

UNIT 9
Reading Drawings and Making Sketches

1-7. Matching. Match the drawing lines with their names by writing the correct letters in the blanks at the left.

_____   1. Hidden line

_____   2. Break line

_____   3. Center line

_____   4. Section line

_____   5. Object line

_____   6. Bend line

_____   7. Dimension line

A

B

C

D

E

F

G

8-17. Multiple Choice. Write the letter of the correct response to each statement or question in the space at the left.

_____   8. A two- or three-view drawing of an object that has all the information needed to make the object is called a
A. pictorial drawing
B. working drawing or blueprint
C. orthographic drawing
D. both B and C

_____   9. In a working drawing, what view appears directly below the top view?
A. front view
B. end view
C. back view
D. bottom view

_____   10. Metric dimensions on working drawings should always be given in what unit of measurement?
A. meters
B. decimeters
C. centimeters
D. millimeters

_____   11. The amount of acceptable variation in a dimension on a working drawing is known as a(n)
A. allowance
B. tolerance
C. variable
D. deviation

(Continued on next page)

_____ 12. An intentional difference in the size of mating parts to provide for a certain kind of fit is called
   A. allowance
   B. tolerance
   C. variation
   D. deviation

_____ 13. The kind of size difference that must be provided for a sliding or running fit is called
   A. positive
   B. negative
   C. plus
   D. minus

_____ 14. The kind of size difference that must be provided for an interference or force fit is called
   A. positive
   B. negative
   C. neutral
   D. normal

_____ 15. What kind of tolerance is indicated by the following dimension?

$$2.250'' [57.15 \text{ mm}] \begin{array}{c} +0.005'' [0.127 \text{ mm}] \\ -0.001'' [0.025 \text{ mm}] \end{array}$$

   A. positive unilateral
   B. negative unilateral
   C. bilateral
   D. none of the above

_____ 16. The part of a drawing that shows the object as if part of it were cut away is called a
   A. section
   B. partial view
   C. sectional view
   D. A or C

_____ 17. A drawing that is made using only a pencil and paper, without the use of drafting instruments, is called a
   A. pictorial drawing
   B. working drawing
   C. blueprint
   D. sketch

18-26. Matching. Match the lettered abbreviations with their numbered meanings by writing the correct letters in the blanks at the left.

_____ 18. Cold-rolled steel

_____ 19. Right-hand

_____ 20. Countersink

_____ 21. Unified National Coarse

_____ 22. Diameter

_____ 23. Threads

_____ 24. Left-hand

_____ 25. Unified National Fine

_____ 26. Radius

A. DIA
B. THDS
C. RH
D. LH
E. R
F. UNC
G. UNF
H. CRS
I. CSK

Name _____

Score _____

UNIT 10
Product Planning

1-5. Multiple Choice. Write the letter of the correct response to each statement or question in the space at the left.

_____   1. Most of the information for making a bill of materials for a product can be found
   A. in catalogs   C. on the pictorial sketch
   B. on the working drawing   D. on specification sheets

_____   2. The material sizes listed on the bill of materials should be which size?
   A. the size of the finished parts   B. the rough size of the metal needed to
                                                make the parts

_____   3. Parts that are the same no matter who makes them or where they are made are called
   A. common parts   C. standard parts
   B. custom parts   D. universal parts

_____   4. Materials such as metal sheets, rods, bars, and tubing that are made to standard sizes
      are called
   A. common stock   C. custom stock
   B. standard stock   D. universal stock

_____   5. The unit of measure normally used by wholesalers in pricing metals is
   A. length   C. weight
   B. volume   D. area

6-9. Short Answer. Solve the following material cost problems. Write your answers in the blanks at the left.

_____   6. Figure the cost of 18′ [5486.4 mm] of ⅜″ [9.5 mm] diameter hot-rolled steel rod that is priced at 48¢ per foot [304.8 mm].

_____   7. What is the cost of 1¼″ [31.8 mm] of 2″ [50.8 mm] diameter aluminum that is priced at $9.50 per foot [304.8 mm]?

_____   8. Calculate the cost of a piece of 24-gage galvanized steel measuring 14″ × 16″ [355.6 × 406.4 mm] that is priced at $1.65 per square foot [$17.76 per square meter].

_____   9. Figure the cost of an aluminum casting weighing 12 ounces [0.34 kg] if cast aluminum is priced at 80¢/lb [1.76/kg].

(Continued on next page)

10-20. Matching. Match the standard shapes with their names by writing the correct letters in the blanks.

———— 10. Round rod

———— 11. I-beam

———— 12. Hexagonal rod

———— 13. Angle iron

———— 14. Square tubing

———— 15. Flat strip

———— 16. Channel iron

———— 17. Square rod

———— 18. Tee iron

———— 19. Round tubing

———— 20. Octagonal rod

A

B

C

D

E

F

G

H

I

J

K

Name _____

Score _____

UNIT 11
Linear Measurement

1-5. Short Answer. On the 6-inch rule shown, five points are marked for reading. Write the correct length for each numbered point in the space provided.

_____ 1.

_____ 2.

_____ 3.

_____ 4.

_____ 5.

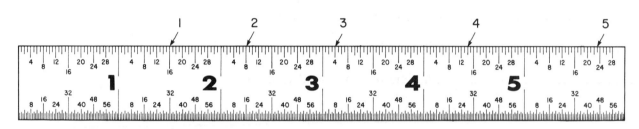

6-10. Short Answer. On the 150-mm rule shown, five points are marked for reading. Write the correct length for each numbered point in the space provided.

_____ 6.

_____ 7.

_____ 8.

_____ 9.

_____ 10.

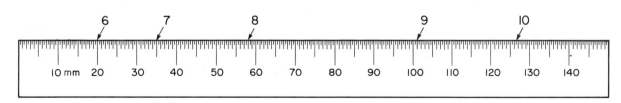

(Continued on next page)

11-24. Short Answer. Write the decimal equivalent, to the nearest thousandth of an inch, of each of the following fractions.

_____ 11. ⅞″

_____ 12. ¾″

_____ 13. ⅝″

_____ 14. ⁹⁄₁₆″

_____ 15. ½″

_____ 16. ⁷⁄₁₆″

_____ 17. ⅜″

_____ 18. ⁵⁄₁₆″

_____ 19. ¼″

_____ 20. ³⁄₁₆″

_____ 21. ⅛″

_____ 22. ¹⁄₁₆″

_____ 23. ¹⁄₃₂″

_____ 24. ¹⁄₆₄″

25-32. Short Answer. Write each of the following dimensions in decimal form.

_____ 25. One and three-quarter inches

_____ 26. Six hundred twenty-five thousandths of an inch

_____ 27. Sixty-two thousandths of an inch

_____ 28. One half-thousandth of an inch

_____ 29. One ten-thousandth of an inch

_____ 30. Twenty-five and four-tenths millimeters

_____ 31. Six and thirty-five hundredths millimeters

_____ 32. Two thousandths of a millimeter

33-44. Short Answer. Using the conversion tables in Unit 11, change the following to the nearest hundredth of a millimeter.

_____ 33. 1″

_____ 34. ¾″

_____ 35. ⅝″

_____ 36. ⁵⁄₁₆″

_____ 37. ⁷⁄₃₂″

_____ 38. ¹⁵⁄₆₄″

_____ 39. 2¼″

_____ 40. 8⅞″

_____ 41. 0.130″

_____ 42. 0.375″

_____ 43. 0.0625″

_____ 44. 1.475″

Name _____

Score _____

UNIT 12
Layout Tools

1-2. Multiple Choice. Write the letter of the correct response to each statement in the space at the left.

_____ 1. The process of marking lines, circles, and arcs on metal surfaces is called
       A. drafting   C. layout work
       B. mechanical drawing   D. designing

_____ 2. A precision flat surface on which a workpiece is placed for accurate marking or measuring is called a
       A. plane surface   C. gage block
       B. surface plate   D. reference plate

3-8. Matching. Match each part of the combination set shown with its name. Write the correct letter in the blank.

_____ 3. Level

_____ 4. Protractor

_____ 5. Blade

_____ 6. Square head

_____ 7. Center head

_____ 8. Scriber

(Continued on next page)

9-21. Matching. Match each layout tool with its name. Write the correct letter in the blank at the left.

_____ 9. Prick punch

_____ 10. Outside caliper

_____ 11. Center punch

_____ 12. Scriber

_____ 13. Trammels

_____ 14. Surface gage

_____ 15. Inside caliper

_____ 16. Dividers

_____ 17. Hermaphrodite calipers

_____ 18. Vernier height gage

_____ 19. Angle plate

_____ 20. Parallel clamp

_____ 21. V-blocks

A

B

C

D

E

F

G

H

I

J

K

L

M

Name _____

Score _____

UNIT 13
Layout Techniques

1-11. Multiple Choice. Write the letter of the correct response to each statement or question in the space at the left.

_____   1. A layout is made from the information given on the
     A. working drawing   C. pictorial drawing
     B. preliminary sketch   D. specification sheets

_____   2. So that a layout on a smooth metal surface may be seen easily, the surface should be coated with
     A. paint   C. layout fluid
     B. chalk   D. ink

_____   3. Before a metal surface is colored for layout, it should be
     A. sanded smooth   C. rubbed clean
     B. machined   D. coated with oil

_____   4. Dried layout fluid can be removed from the metal by
     A. washing with alcohol   C. rubbing with steel wool
     B. washing with water   D. A or C

_____   5. For the most accurate measurement, how should a steel rule be placed on the workpiece?
     A. with its broad surface lying on the workpiece   C. with the edge of the rule in contact with the workpiece
     B. angled at about 45 degrees   D. any of the above

_____   6. Lines, circles, and arcs can be made to last longer on a layout by
     A. using layout fluid   C. center punching them
     B. prick punching them   D. using chalk

_____   7. Lines that are square with, parallel to, or 45 degrees to a straight workpiece edge can be quickly laid out with a
     A. bevel protractor   C. combination square
     B. center square   D. solid square

_____   8. Lines of any angle desired can be laid out from a straight workpiece edge with a
     A. combination square   C. center square
     B. bevel protractor   D. compass

_____   9. The center of the end of a round bar can be found most quickly by using a
     A. bevel protractor   C. combination square
     B. center gage   D. center square

(Continued on next page)

_____ 10. To scribe a circle with a diameter of 1¹⁄₁₂″ [38.1 mm], how far apart should the divider points be?
 A. 1½″ [38.1 mm]   C. ⅝″ [15.88 mm]
 B. ¾″ [19.05 mm]   D. ⅜″ [9.5 mm]

_____ 11. To scribe a circle, one point of the divider should be placed on a mark made at the circle's center with a
 A. prick punch   C. scriber
 B. center punch   D. drill

12-17. Layout. Using a compass and a straightedge, do the following layout exercises:

12. Make a 1″ [25.4 mm] circle and divide its circumference into six equal parts.

13. Find the center of this circle:

14. Find the center of this arc:

15. Lay out a line parallel to and ½″ [12.7 mm] above the line given below.

16. Lay out a perpendicular line through point A on the line below.

A

17. Bisect the angle given.

34

UNIT 14
Micrometers and Verniers

1-18. Multiple Choice. Write the letter of the correct response to each statement or question in the space at the left.

_____ 1. A plain inch micrometer measures to what part of an inch?
  A. 0.1″   C. 0.001″
  B. 0.01″   D. 0.0001″

_____ 2. A plain metric micrometer measures to what part of a millimeter?
  A. 0.1 mm   C. 0.001 mm
  B. 0.01 mm   D. 0.0001 mm

_____ 3. A micrometer that is used to measure the diameter of round objects and the thickness of flat pieces is called a(n)
  A. plain micrometer   C. caliper micrometer
  B. vernier micrometer   D. outside micrometer

_____ 4. A micrometer that is used to measure screw threads is called a(n)
  A. outside micrometer   C. inside micrometer
  B. screw thread micrometer   D. depth micrometer

_____ 5. A micrometer that is used to measure the diameter of holes is called a(n)
  A. depth micrometer   C. inside micrometer
  B. outside micrometer   D. hole micrometer

_____ 6. Name the micrometer that is used to measure how deep a hole, slot, or groove is.
  A. hole micrometer   C. outside micrometer
  B. depth micrometer   D. inside micrometer

_____ 7. The smallest size that a 2″ micrometer will measure is
  A. 2″   B. 1″

_____ 8. What part on some micrometers helps different users apply the same pressure when taking measurements?
  A. ratchet stop   C. pressure gage
  B. friction stop   D. A or B

_____ 9. The part of the micrometer on which the 0.001″ graduation marks are located is the
  A. frame   C. thimble
  B. barrel or sleeve   D. spindle

(Continued on next page)

_____ 10. The part of an inch micrometer on which the 40 equal spaces of 0.025″ are marked
is the
A. frame   C. thimble
B. barrel or sleeve   D. spindle

_____ 11. How many threads per inch are there on an inch micrometer spindle or measuring
screw?
A. 10   C. 40
B. 25   D. 100

_____ 12. How many turns of a metric micrometer thimble are needed to move it one milli-
meter?
A. 1   C. 3
B. 2   D. 4

_____ 13. A vernier inch micrometer measures to what part of an inch?
A. 0.1″   C. 0.001″
B. 0.01″   D. 0.0001″

_____ 14. A vernier metric micrometer measures to what part of a millimeter?
A. 0.1 mm   C. 0.001 mm
B. 0.01 mm   D. 0.002 mm

_____ 15. To test the accuracy of a 2″ micrometer,
A. close it to see if it reads zero   C. measure a 2″ gage block or standard
B. measure a 1″ gage block or standard   D. B or C

_____ 16. Inch vernier calipers measure accurately to what part of an inch?
A. ¹/₂₅th   C. ¹/₁₀₀₀th
B. ¹/₅₀th   D. ¹/₁₀,₀₀₀th

_____ 17. One type of metric vernier caliper measures accurately to 0.05 mm. The other type
measures accurately to
A. 0.02 mm   C. 0.001 mm
B. 0.01 mm   D. 0.002 mm

_____ 18. The vernier protractor measures accurately to what part of a degree?
A. ½   C. ¹/₁₀th
B. ¼   D. ¹/₁₂th

19-30. Short Answer. Set a micrometer to the following sizes and have each reading checked by
your instructor or an assigned classmate. Then repeat the exercise using a vernier caliper or height
gage. Check off each reading as you complete it correctly by making a mark in the blank.

_____ 19. 0.025″   _____ 25. 0.4297″

_____ 20. 0.100″   _____ 26. 1 mm

_____ 21. 0.250″   _____ 27. 0.5 mm

_____ 22. 0.562″   _____ 28. 6.35 mm

_____ 23. 0.875″   _____ 29. 12.71 mm

_____ 24. 0.3333″   _____ 30. 19.05 mm

Name _____

Score _____

UNIT 15
Hand Sawing

1-14. Multiple Choice. Write the letter of the correct response to each statement or question in the space at the left.

_____ 1. Which type of hand hacksaw blade is less likely to break?
A. all hard
B. semi-flexible
C. flexible
D. none of the above

_____ 2. Which one of the following **is not** a standard hand hacksaw blade length?
A. 8″ [200 mm]
B. 10″ [250 mm]
C. 12″ [300 mm]
D. 14″ [355 mm]

_____ 3. Hand hacksaw blades for cutting metal less than 1/16″ [1.6 mm] thick should have how many teeth?
A. 32 teeth per inch [0.8 mm pitch]
B. 24 teeth per inch [1 mm pitch]
C. 18 teeth per inch [1.4 mm pitch]
D. 14 teeth per inch [1.8 mm pitch]

_____ 4. Hand hacksaw blades for cutting metal 1/4″ to 1″ [6.35 to 25.4 mm] thick should have how many teeth?
A. 32 teeth per inch [0.8 mm pitch]
B. 24 teeth per inch [1 mm pitch]
C. 18 teeth per inch [1.4 mm pitch]
D. 14 teeth per inch [1.8 mm pitch]

_____ 5. Two kinds of tooth set patterns used on hand hacksaw blades are
A. alternate and raker
B. raker and wavy
C. wavy and alternate
D. alternate and skip

_____ 6. The teeth of a hand hacksaw blade, properly installed, should point
A. away from the handle
B. toward the handle

_____ 7. A rattling noise caused by rapid vibration of a loose tool or workpiece while cutting is called
A. wiggle
B. drumming
C. knock
D. chatter

_____ 8. To avoid stripping of hacksaw blade teeth while cutting, what minimum number of teeth should always be in contact with the workpiece?
A. 1
B. 2
C. 3
D. 4

(Continued on next page)

9. When sawing metal that is thinner than the space between two teeth, how can stripping of teeth be prevented?
   A. Clamp the metal between two thicker pieces of metal or hard wood.
   B. Use a dull hacksaw blade.
   C. Place the blade almost parallel to the metal surface while cutting.
   D. A or C

10. The hand hacksaw is intended to cut on the
    A. forward stroke
    B. backward stroke

11. About how many cutting strokes per minute should be made with a hand hacksaw?
    A. 30
    B. 40
    C. 50
    D. 60

12. If a new blade must be used to finish a hacksaw cut, what is the best procedure to use?
    A. Make a new cut next to the old one.
    B. Put the new blade in the old cut and continue cutting.
    C. Turn the piece over and start a new cut from the other side.
    D. A or C

13. What hand saw is best to use for cutting curved shapes in thin metal?
    A. hacksaw
    B. coping saw
    C. jeweler's saw
    D. sabre saw

14. Which direction should the teeth of a jeweler's saw point?
    A. toward the handle
    B. away from the handle

Name _____

Score _____

UNIT 16
Cold Chisels

1-4. Matching. Match the names of cold chisels with their uses. Write the correct letters in the blanks at the left.

_____ 1. Flat cold chisel

_____ 2. Cape chisel

_____ 3. Diamond-point chisel

_____ 4. Round-nose chisel

A. Cutting V-shaped grooves and square corners.
B. Cutting sheet metal, small bars, rivets, and flat surfaces.
C. Cutting rounded corners and grooves.
D. Cutting narrow, flat-bottom grooves.

5-11. Multiple Choice. Write the letter of the correct response to each statement or question in the space at the left.

_____ 5. The cutting edge of a cold chisel is sloped like a(n)
    A. inclined plane   C. center punch
    B. wedge   D. cylinder

_____ 6. For ordinary work, the angle of the cutting edge of a flat cold chisel should be
    A. 30 degrees   C. 60 degrees
    B. 45 degrees   D. 90 degrees

_____ 7. A tool commonly used to test the cutting edge angle of a cold chisel is the
    A. center square   C. protractor
    B. center gage   D. B or C

_____ 8. Which kind of cold chisel cutting edge gives the better shearing action?
    A. slightly curved   B. straight

_____ 9. If the head of a cold chisel becomes mushroomed, what tool is used to reshape it?
    A. another cold chisel   C. a grinder
    B. a file   D. a hammer

_____ 10. To chisel safely, protect yourself from flying chips by wearing
    A. gloves   C. an apron
    B. a respirator   D. goggles

_____ 11. Cutting metal by using the vise jaws and a flat chisel so that together they act like a pair of scissors is called
    A. snipping   C. slicing
    B. shearing   D. cutting

Name _____

Score _____

UNIT 17
Files and Filing

1-18. Multiple Choice. Write the letter of the correct response to each statement or question in the space at the left.

_____ 1. What material are files made of?
A. gray cast iron
B. wrought iron
C. white cast iron
D. hardened steel

_____ 2. The part of the file that fits into the handle is the
A. point
B. spike
C. heel
D. tang

_____ 3. The file's edge that has no teeth is called the
A. bevel edge
B. smooth edge
C. safe edge
D. tooth-free edge

_____ 4. What part of a wooden file handle keeps it from splitting?
A. ferrule
B. ring
C. collar
D. cuff

_____ 5. Which kind of file is thinner or narrower at the point than at the heel?
A. warding
B. knife
C. tapered
D. wedge

_____ 6. A file that is the same thickness and width from the point to the heel is called a
A. normal file
B. blunt file
C. standard file
D. straight file

_____ 7. The length of a file is the distance from the point to the
A. heel
B. end of the tang

_____ 8. A file with a single row of teeth is called a
A. one-row file
B. one-cut file
C. single-cut file
D. single-row file

_____ 9. A file with two rows of teeth that cross each other is called a
A. two-cut file
B. two-row file
C. double-row file
D. double-cut file

_____ 10. How does the size of a file affect its coarseness?
A. It has no affect.
B. Coarseness increases with length.
C. Coarseness decreases with length.
D. Coarseness increases with width.

_____ 11. Small files measuring four to six inches [100-150 mm] in length and usually sold in sets are called
  A. jeweler's files   C. needle files
  B. toolmaker's files   D. A and B

_____ 12. Files made especially for tool, die, and mold work are called
  A. rotary files   C. rifflers
  B. jeweler's files   D. contour files

_____ 13. Files that are used in revolving holders driven by electric or air-powered motors are called
  A. spinning files   C. rotary files
  B. revolving files   D. rotating files

_____ 14. The kind of filing done with the file held parallel to the surface but at a 45-degree angle is called
  A. cross-filing   C. angular filing
  B. draw-filing   D. square filing

_____ 15. The kind of filing done with the file held parallel to the surface but at a 90-degree angle is called
  A. cross-filing   C. square filing
  B. draw-filing   D. angular filing

_____ 16. Why should the scale on cast iron be removed before filing?
  A. so it won't clog the file   B. so it won't dull the file

_____ 17. A tool used for cleaning a file is called a file
  A. scraper   C. card and brush
  B. cleaner   D. comb

_____ 18. To help kccp metal from sticking between the file teeth, the file should be
  A. oiled   C. kept clean and dry
  B. rubbed with chalk   D. brushed often

19-24. Matching. Files range from coarse to smooth. Label the file classifications below from A to F, with A being the smoothest and F the coarsest.

_____ 19. Coarse

_____ 20. Smooth

_____ 21. Second-cut

_____ 22. Rough

_____ 23. Dead smooth

_____ 24. Bastard

(Continued on next page)

25-32. Matching. Match the names of the files with their uses or descriptions by writing the correct letters in the blanks.

_____ 25. Round file

_____ 26. Hand file

_____ 27. Curved-cut file

_____ 28. Three-square file

_____ 29. Mill file

_____ 30. Pillar file

_____ 31. Rasp

_____ 32. Half-round file

A. Used for draw-filing and finishing cuts.
B. Also known as a rat-tail file.
C. Used for filing keyways, slots, and grooves.
D. Has one flat surface and one curved surface.
E. Used for filing corners and angles less than 90 degrees.
F. Always has one safe edge; used to finish flat surfaces.
G. Specially made for filing soft metals.
H. Specially made for shaping wood and similar materials.

Name _____

Score _____

UNIT 18
Wrought Metal Bending

1-11. Multiple Choice. Write the letter of the correct response to each statement or question in the space at the left.

_____ 1. Many wrought metals up to which thickness can be bent cold?
   A. ⅛″ [3.2 mm]   C. ⅜″ [9.5 mm]
   B. ¼″ [6.35 mm]   D. ½″ [12.7 mm]

_____ 2. The kind of iron widely used by early blacksmiths for making useful and decorative objects was
   A. cast iron   C. ductile iron
   B. malleable iron   D. wrought iron

_____ 3. Which one of the following metals **is not** widely used for making present-day wrought metal products?
   A. copper   C. aluminum
   B. wrought iron   D. hot-rolled low-carbon steel

_____ 4. The recommended bend allowance for soft metals is what fraction of the metal's thickness?
   A. ¼   C. ½
   B. ⅓   D. ⅔

_____ 5. The recommended bend allowance for hard metals is what fraction of the metal's thickness?
   A. ¼   C. ½
   B. ⅓   D. ⅔

_____ 6. To figure the length of a metal piece needed for a curve or a ring, calculate or measure the length of its
   A. outside surface   C. centerline
   B. inside surface   D. none of the above

_____ 7. A simple mechanical device that must be clamped in a vise when used for making curved bends of any shape is called a
   A. universal bending jig   C. universal bending machine
   B. bending fork   D. A or B

_____ 8. When long sections of metal bars or strips are twisted, they can be kept in line if they are twisted
   A. hot   C. inside a close-fitting pipe
   B. cold   D. all of the above

(Continued on next page)

_____ 9. Hand- or power-operated machines for bending metal bars and tubing are called
   A. bending jigs
   B. universal bending jigs
   C. universal bending machines
   D. metal formers

_____ 10. Hammering wrought metal surfaces to give them a roughened texture is called
   A. decorating
   B. patterning
   C. peening
   D. pounding

_____ 11. A protective coating usually used on wrought iron or wrought steel products is
   A. clear lacquer
   B. flat black paint
   C. white paint
   D. zinc

12-15. Short Answer. List four methods of assembling wrought metal products.

12. _____

13. _____

14. _____

15. _____

Name _____

Score _____

UNIT 19
Screw Threads

1-15. Multiple Choice. Write the letter of the correct answer to each statement or question in the space at the left.

_____ 1. The threads on most standard threaded fasteners are made on cold-heading machines with
      A. ordinary thread-cutting dies   C. flat thread-rolling dies
      B. round thread-rolling dies   D. single-point threading tools

_____ 2. The largest diameter of a straight external or internal screw thread is called the
      A. outside diameter   C. inside diameter
      B. major diameter   D. minor diameter

_____ 3. The smallest diameter of a straight external or internal screw thread is called the
      A. outside diameter   C. minor diameter
      B. major diameter   D. inside diameter

_____ 4. The diameter of a screw thread that determines the fit or clearance between mating threads is the
      A. major diameter   C. pitch diameter
      B. minor diameter   D. actual outside diameter

_____ 5. The distance from a point on one thread to a corresponding point on the next thread is called the
      A. lead   C. travel
      B. pitch   D. gap

_____ 6. Two ways to measure the pitch of screw threads are
      A. with a plain micrometer and a screw   C. with a rule and a plain micrometer
           pitch gage   D. with a screw pitch gage and a rule
      B. with dividers and a micrometer

_____ 7. The thread form that was first adopted by most American industries was the
      A. American National   C. United States Standard
      B. Unified National   D. ISO Metric

_____ 8. The form of screw thread most widely used in the United States today is the
      A. American National   C. United States Standard
      B. Unified   D. ISO Metric

_____ 9. The thread angle of the Unified Screw Thread is
      A. 30°   C. 60°
      B. 45°   D. 90°

(Continued on next page)

_____ 10. The class of a Unified National Thread has to do with the
A. pitch of the thread
B. fit of the thread
C. smoothness of the finish on the threads
D. lead of the thread

_____ 11. A 29-degree thread used mostly on machine tools is the
A. ISO Metric
B. Unified National
C. Acme
D. pipe thread

_____ 12. The type of pipe thread used for general-purpose jobs that require a low-pressure seal is the American National Standard
A. Taper Pipe Thread
B. Straight Pipe Thread
C. Railing Joint Taper Pipe Thread
D. Dryseal Taper Pipe Thread

_____ 13. ISO Inch and ISO Metric threads are not interchangeable because of differences in their
A. thread angle
B. diameters
C. pitches
D. B and C

_____ 14. Which ISO Metric thread is commonly used on metric fasteners?
A. coarse pitch
B. fine pitch
C. constant pitch
D. variable pitch

_____ 15. How are ISO Metric threads designated on working drawings?
A. with the letters ISO
B. with the letter I
C. with the letter M
D. with the letter m

16-17. Short Answer. Write your answers in the blanks at the left.

_____ 16. What is the thread designation for a coarse metric thread of 20 mm diameter and 2.5 mm pitch?

_____ 17. What is the thread designation for a fine metric thread of 12 mm diameter and 1.25 mm pitch?

Name _____

Score _____

UNIT 20
External Threading with Dies

1-7. Multiple Choice. Write the letter of the correct answer to each statement or question in the space at the left.

_____   1. Cutting threads by hand on a round bar is done with a tool called a
                A. threading tap   C. thread chaser
                B. threading die   D. thread cutter

_____   2. A set of taps and dies is called a
                A. tap-and-die set   C. thread-cutting kit
                B. threading set   D. screw plate

_____   3. The tool for holding and turning the threading die is called a
                A. die wrench   C. diestock
                B. die lever   D. die holder

_____   4. To make it easier to start a threading die, the end of the rod should be
                A. beveled   C. squared off
                B. rounded off   D. reduced in diameter

_____   5. The starting side of a die
                A. has smaller teeth   C. has straight teeth
                B. has three or four tapered teeth   D. has oversized teeth

_____   6. Why is it recommended to back up the die every two or three turns when threading?
                A. to break the chip into small pieces   C. to help make a smoother thread
                B. to make it easier to turn the die   D. both A and C

_____   7. A good cutting fluid to use for threading steel is
                A. soluble oil   C. sulfurized mineral oil
                B. inactive mineral oil   D. all of the above

8-11. Short Answer. List four ways of measuring an external thread for correct pitch diameter or fit.

8. _____

9. _____

10. _____

11. _____

Name _____

Score _____

UNIT 21
Internal Threading with Taps

1-10. Multiple Choice. Write the letter of the correct answer to each statement or question in the space to the left.

_____ 1. A tool used to cut threads inside a hole, such as in a nut, is called a
A. tap   B. die

_____ 2. A style of tap that should be backed up a turn every two or three turns in order to break the chip into small pieces is the
A. gun tap   C. helical-fluted tap
B. hand tap   D. cam ground tap

_____ 3. A style of tap that shoots the chip ahead of it and is used for tapping through holes is the
A. gun tap   C. hand tap
B. serial tap   D. helical-fluted tap

_____ 4. A style of tap that lifts the chips out of the hole and is used for tapping of blind holes is the
A. gun tap   C. hand tap
B. serial tap   D. helical-fluted tap

_____ 5. A style of tap designed especially for use in tough materials is the
A. gun tap   C. hand tap
B. serial tap   D. helical-fluted tap

_____ 6. A style of tap that has no flutes and does not produce chips is the
A. hand tap   C. gun tap
B. thread-forming tap   D. serial tap

_____ 7. A tap drill is
A. a special drill for a certain size tap   B. an ordinary drill that is the correct size for a certain size tap

_____ 8. The tool that is used to hold and turn a tap by hand is the tap
A. wrench   C. stock
B. holder   D. tool

_____ 9. A tool made for removing broken taps is the
A. tap remover   C. screw extractor
B. tap extractor   D. tap eliminator

_____ 10. Threaded steel bushings that are used to repair damaged or stripped threads are called thread

    A. rings
    B. inserts
    C. plugs
    D. collars

11-17. Matching. Match the taps shown with their names by writing the correct letters in the blanks.

_____ 11. Gun tap

_____ 12. Taper tap

_____ 13. Helical-fluted tap

_____ 14. Serial tap

_____ 15. Plug tap

_____ 16. Thread-forming tap

_____ 17. Bottoming tap

18-20. Short Answer. A tap is marked ¼-20 UNC. Explain what the markings mean in the space provided.

18. ¼: _____

19. 20: _____

20. UNC: _____

(Continued on next page)

21-26. Short Answer. List six causes of broken taps.

21. _____

22. _____

23. _____

24. _____

25. _____

26. _____

27-29. Short Answer. Look up the correct tap drill size for each of the following taps. Write the sizes in the blanks at the left.

_____ 27. ¼-20 UNC tap

_____ 28. ⅜-24 UNF tap

_____ 29. M8 × 1 tap

Name _____

Score _____

UNIT 22
Fits and Fitting

1-7. Multiple Choice. Write the letter of the correct answer to each statement or question in the space to the left.

_____ 1. Preparing mating parts so that they will assemble correctly is called
   A. bench work   C. fitting
   B. scraping   D. reworking

_____ 2. The motion of a piston in a cylinder is an example of what kind of fit?
   A. running   C. locational
   B. sliding   D. force

_____ 3. A shaft rotating in a bearing is an example of what kind of fit?
   A. running   C. locational
   B. sliding   D. force

_____ 4. When gears or pulleys are assembled on shafts by pressing them together, what kind of fit is used?
   A. running   C. locational
   B. sliding   D. force

_____ 5. A kind of force fit that can be used when parts cannot be pressed together is the
   A. expansion fit   C. vacuum fit
   B. shrink fit   D. squeeze fit

_____ 6. The difference between a shaft diameter and the diameter of the hole it is to fit is called the
   A. tolerance   C. difference
   B. allowance   D. margin

_____ 7. Very thin layers of metal used to separate two halves of a plain bearing are called
   A. leaves   C. shims
   B. foils   D. separators

(Continued on next page)

8-11. Short Answer. Name four cutting operations sometimes used to get parts to fit together correctly.

8. _____

9. _____

10. _____

11. _____

12-14. Short Answer. Name occupations that require skill in fitting.

12. _____

13. _____

14. _____

15-18. Short Answer. List four things that affect the allowance provided for various fits.

15. _____

16. _____

17. _____

18. _____

Name _____

Score _____

UNIT 23
Scrapers and Scraping

1-4. Matching. Match the scrapers shown with their names by writing the correct letters in the blanks at the left.

_____   1. Flat scraper

_____   2. Hook scraper

_____   3. Three-cornered scraper

_____   4. Half-round scraper

A

B

C

D

5-13. Multiple Choice. Write the letter of the correct answer to each statement or question in the space to the left.

_____   5. Shaving or paring off thin slices or flakes of metal with a hand tool in order to make a fine, smooth surface is called
   A. fitting   C. scraping
   B. deburring   D. filing

_____   6. Two scrapers used for scraping flat surfaces are the
   A. flat and three-cornered   C. hook and flat
   B. three-cornered and half-round   D. hook and three-cornered

_____   7. Two scrapers used for scraping curved surfaces are the
   A. flat and half-round   C. hook and flat
   B. three-cornered and half-round   D. hook and three-cornered

_____   8. Which scraper is used for removing sharp edges from holes?
   A. hook   C. flat
   B. three-cornered   D. half-round

_____   9. What tool is used to find the high spots on flat work during the scraping operation?
   A. surface plate   C. flat scraper
   B. dial indicator   D. vernier height gage

(Continued on next page)

_____ 10. The name of the blue paint that is used on top of the surface plate is
A. blue vitriol   C. Prussian blue
B. layout fluid   D. Russian blue

_____ 11. If the blue paint is put on the surface plate too thick, the piece to be scraped will have
A. only the high spots marked   C. the whole surface marked
B. only the low spots marked   D. none of the above

_____ 12. For scraping a round bearing, the blue paint should be put on
A. the bearing   B. the shaft

_____ 13. An imitation of frost, patchwork, or checkerboard design made by scraping is called
A. flowering   C. frosting
B. cross-hatching   D. both A and C

Name _____

Score _____

UNIT 24
Assembly Tools

1-6. Multiple Choice. Write the letter of the correct answer to each statement or question in the space to the left.

_____ 1. The size of a screwdriver is measured by
A. the length of its blade   B. its overall length

_____ 2. A two-bladed screwdriver that has its blades bent at 90 degrees to its handle is called
A. a bent screwdriver   C. an offset screwdriver
B. a 90-degree screwdriver   D. a square-bend screwdriver

_____ 3. When using an adjustable wrench, which direction should the jaws point?
A. in the direction opposite to the di-   B. in the same direction that the handle
   rection the handle is to be pulled   is to be pulled

_____ 4. Hammers that are made of lead, copper, and other soft metals are called
A. mallets   C. safe hammers
B. soft hammers   D. metal hammers

_____ 5. Hammers that are made of wood, leather, rubber, or plastic are called
A. mallets   C. safe hammers
B. soft hammers   D. finishing hammers

_____ 6. The size of a machinist's vise is determined by the
A. weight of the vise   C. width of its jaws
B. maximum distance it can open   D. a combination of B and C

7-9. Matching. Match the pliers shown below with their names by writing the correct letters in the blanks at the left.

_____ 7. Side-cutting pliers

_____ 8. Combination pliers

_____ 9. Round-nose pliers

(Continued on next page)

10-19. Matching. Match the wrenches shown below with their names. Write the correct letters in the blanks to the left.

_____ 10. Open-end wrench

_____ 11. Socket wrench

_____ 12. Spanner wrench

_____ 13. Hexagonal wrench

_____ 14. Adjustable end wrench

_____ 15. Vise-grip® wrench

_____ 16. Pipe wrench

_____ 17. Monkey wrench

_____ 18. Box wrench

_____ 19. Torque wrench

20-22. Matching. Match the punches shown below with their names by writing the correct letters in the blanks at the left.

_____ 20. Pin punch

_____ 21. Drift punch

_____ 22. Transfer punch

23-26. Matching. Match the clamps shown below with their names by writing the correct letters in the blanks at the left.

_____ 23. Toggle clamp

_____ 24. C-clamp

_____ 25. Spring clamp

_____ 26. Toolmaker's parallel clamp

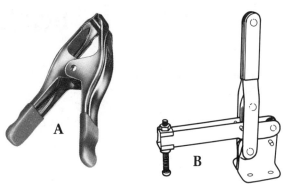

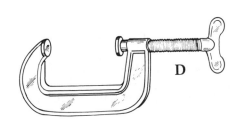

Name _____

Score _____

UNIT 25
Fasteners

1-17. Multiple Choice. Write the letter of the correct answer to each statement or question in the space at the left.

_____ 1. The length of bolts and screws does not include the length of the head **except** for what head type?
A. round
B. flat
C. square
D. hexagonal

_____ 2. What type of fastener is used for fastening a wooden part to metal?
A. machine bolt
B. lag screw
C. carriage bolt
D. tap bolt

_____ 3. What type of fastener is used to fasten a metal part to wood?
A. machine bolt
B. lag screw
C. carriage bolt
D. cap screw

_____ 4. Screws that have cone, dog, flat, cup, and round points are called
A. machine screws
B. wood screws
C. cap screws
D. setscrews

_____ 5. The included angle of flat-head screws is
A. 60 degrees
B. 82 degrees
C. 90 degrees
D. 118 degrees

_____ 6. What kind of nut is used to keep another nut from loosening by vibration?
A. lock nut
B. jam nut
C. check nut
D. all of the above

_____ 7. What kind of washer is used under a nut to keep it from loosening?
A. jam washer
B. lock washer
C. check washer
D. plain washer

_____ 8. A circular fastener installed in a hole or on a shaft, usually in a ring groove, and used to hold a part in proper position is called a
A. spring ring
B. holding ring
C. retaining ring
D. positioning ring

_____ 9. Screws that cut or form their own threads when installed are called
A. self-threading screws
B. threadless screws
C. threading screws
D. thread-making screws

_____ 10. Drive screws are installed with a
A. hammer
B. screwdriver
C. hex wrench
D. socket wrench

_____ 11. The sizes of tinner's rivets are designated by the weight of how many of that size?
A. 1   C. 100
B. 10   D. 1000

_____ 12. The hole made for a rivet should provide a
A. drive fit   C. loose fit
B. snug fit   D. sloppy fit

_____ 13. Rivets should not be spaced closer together than how many times the rivet diameter?
A. 2   C. 4
B. 3   D. 6

_____ 14. What tool is used to form the end of a rivet into a smooth, round head?
A. riveting hammer   C. rivet set
B. ball-peen hammer   D. rivet punch

_____ 15. Very large rivets, such as those used to rivet structural steel beams, are riveted while they are
A. cold   C. hot
B. warm   D. temperature makes no difference

_____ 16. Pull-stem blind rivets are commonly known as
A. snap rivets   C. explosive rivets
B. bang rivets   D. Pop® rivets

_____ 17. A broken bolt may be removed from a hole with a
A. bolt extractor   C. bolt eliminator
B. bolt remover   D. screw extractor

18-23. Matching. Match the bolts and screws pictured with their names by writing the correct letters in the blanks at the left.

_____ 18. Machine bolt

_____ 19. Stud bolt

_____ 20. Lag screw

_____ 21. Thumb screw

_____ 22. Machine screw

_____ 23. Cap screw

(Continued on next page)

24-26. Matching. Match the types of keys with their names by writing the correct letters in the blanks at the left.

_____ 24. Woodruff

_____ 25. Square

_____ 26. Gib-head

27-32. Matching. Match the types of rivet heads with their names by writing the correct letters in the blanks at the left.

_____ 27. Cone

_____ 28. Flat

_____ 29. Round or button

_____ 30. Truss

_____ 31. Steeple

_____ 32. Countersunk

33-35. Short Answer. Name three kinds of pins used for holding mechanical parts together.

33. _____

34. _____

35. _____

36-39. Short Answer. Name four common kinds of metals from which rivets are made.

36. _____

37. _____

38. _____

39. _____

40-41. Short Answer. Name two types of blind rivets other than the pull-stem type.

40. _____

41. _____

Name _____

Score _____

UNIT 26
Welding

1-36. Multiple Choice. Write the letter of the correct response to each statement or question in the space to the left.

_____ 1. When heat alone is used to melt and flow metal together, the process is known as
   A. soldering
   B. brazing
   C. pressure welding
   D. fusion welding

_____ 2. Welding by heating and then forcing the pieces together is called
   A. fusion welding
   B. pressure welding
   C. inertia welding
   D. dynamic welding

_____ 3. Arc welding can produce temperatures as high as
   A. 20,000° F [11,093° C]
   B. 10,000° F [5538° C]
   C. 5000° F [2760° C]
   D. 1000° F [538° C]

_____ 4. Unless protective clothing is worn, arc welding will cause skin burns much like that obtained from
   A. wind
   B. rain
   C. the sun
   D. rubbing

_____ 5. Which is normal for direct current electric-arc welding in the flat position?
   A. straight polarity
   B. reverse polarity

_____ 6. To which side of the power supply should the arc-welding electrode holder be connected for straight polarity?
   A. positive
   B. negative

_____ 7. A welding electrode that comes covered with materials that melt to protect the weld metal from the air during shielded metal arc welding is called a
   A. covered electrode
   B. coated electrode
   C. shielded electrode
   D. jacketed electrode

_____ 8. The form of arc welding that uses flux-coated welding rods is called
   A. shielded metal arc welding
   B. gas metal arc welding
   C. submerged arc welding
   D. gas tungsten arc welding

_____ 9. What is the approximate tensile strength of an E6013 electrode?
   A. 6000 psi [41.4 MPa]
   B. 13,000 psi [89.6 MPa]
   C. 60,000 psi [413.7 MPa]
   D. 130,000 psi [896.3 MPa]

(Continued on next page)

10. When arc welding, at what angle should the electrode be slanted in the direction of travel when measured from a position vertical to the workpiece?
   A. 5-10 degrees
   B. 5-15 degrees
   C. 10-20 degrees
   D. 15-30 degrees

11. A weld bead made without weaving the electrode side to side is called a
   A. tack weld
   B. runner bead
   C. stringer bead
   D. nonwoven bead

12. For production welding, shielded metal arc welding has been largely replaced by which welding process?
   A. gas tungsten arc welding
   B. gas metal arc welding
   C. submerged arc welding
   D. spot welding

13. The arc welding process used widely for welding magnesium, aluminum, copper, and stainless steel is
   A. submerged arc welding
   B. gas metal arc welding
   C. shielded metal arc welding
   D. gas tungsten arc welding

14. Gases such as helium and argon, which are used to shield the liquid metal during arc welding, are called
   A. inert gases
   B. oxidizing gases
   C. fuel gases
   D. carburizing gases

15. Spot welding is a form of welding known as
   A. flow welding
   B. resistance welding
   C. forge welding
   D. gas welding

16. The most common form of gas welding uses the gases
   A. acetylene and air
   B. acetylene and hydrogen
   C. hydrogen and oxygen
   D. acetylene and oxygen

17. The flame from an oxyacetylene welding torch burns at about
   A. 3000° F [1649° C]
   B. 6000° F [3316° C]
   C. 8000° F [4427° C]
   D. 10,000° F [5538° C]

18. The metal that is melted from the pieces being joined during welding is called the
   A. filler metal
   B. weld metal
   C. project metal
   D. base metal

19. Additional metal added to the welded joint is called
   A. filler metal
   B. weld metal
   C. project metal
   D. base metal

20. When a tank is full, oxygen tank pressure can be as high as
   A. 250 psi [1.7 MPa]
   B. 800 psi [5.5 MPa]
   C. 2200 psi [15.2 MPa]
   D. 6000 psi [41.4 MPa]

21. When an acetylene tank is full, the pressure is about
   A. 250 psi [1.7 MPa]
   B. 800 psi [5.5 MPa]
   C. 2200 psi [15.2 MPa]
   D. 6000 psi [41.4 MPa]

22. How far should an oxygen tank valve be opened?
   A. ¼ turn
   B. ½ turn
   C. one turn
   D. all the way

_____ 23. How far should an acetylene tank valve be opened?
A. ¼ turn
B. ½ turn
C. one turn
D. all the way

_____ 24. What devices control the welding gas pressure delivered to the welding torch?
A. tank valves
B. torch valves
C. gas pressure regulators
D. all of the above

_____ 25. Acetylene gas is unstable when compressed at pressures higher than
A. 5 psi [34.5 kPa]
B. 15 psi [103 kPa]
C. 150 psi [1.0 MPa]
D. 250 psi [1.7 MPa]

_____ 26. What color hose is always used to connect the acetylene regulator to the welding torch?
A. black
B. red
C. green
D. orange

_____ 27. What oxyacetylene torch tip size is recommended for welding metal ⅛″ [3.2 mm] thick?
A. #3
B. #4
C. #5
D. #7

_____ 28. To light an oxyacetylene torch, how far should the acetylene torch valve be opened?
A. ¼ turn
B. ⅓ turn
C. ½ turn
D. ⅔ turn

_____ 29. An oxyacetylene torch should never be lighted with a
A. torch lighter
B. spark lighter
C. match
D. friction lighter

_____ 30. For most welds, what kind of oxyacetylene flame is used?
A. oxidizing
B. carburizing
C. neutral
D. none of the above

_____ 31. A flame that is burning too much acetylene is called
A. neutral
B. carburizing
C. oxidizing
D. all of the above

_____ 32. The tip of the welding torch should form an angle with the workpiece of about how many degrees?
A. 90
B. 60
C. 45
D. 30

_____ 33. For a right-handed person, gas welding from right to left is called
A. forehand technique
B. backhand technique
C. sidehand technique
D. it has no name

_____ 34. To turn off a lighted oxyacetylene torch, which torch valve should be closed first?
A. acetylene
B. oxygen

(Continued on next page)

_____ 35. What is the source of the welding heat for laser welding?
   A. a concentrated beam of electrons   C. a concentrated beam of light
   B. friction   D. a concentrated beam of inert gas

_____ 36. What is the source of welding heat for inertia welding?
   A. a concentrated beam of electrons   C. a concentrated beam of light
   B. friction   D. a concentrated beam of inert gas

37-38. Short Answer. Name the two kinds of electric current used for arc welding.

37. _____

38. _____

39-40. Short Answer. Name two methods of starting an arc with a coated electrode.

39. _____

40. _____

41-45. Short Answer. Name the five basic kinds of joints used in welding. Make a small sketch of each.

41. _____

42. _____

43. _____

44. _____

45. _____

46-49. Short Answer. Name the four basic welding positions.

46. _____

47. _____

48. _____

49. _____

50-53. Short Answer. Name four advanced welding processes.

50. _____

51. _____

52. _____

53. _____

Name _____

Score _____

UNIT 27
Soldering and Brazing

1-16. Multiple Choice. Write the letter of the correct answer to each statement or question in the space to the left.

_____ 1. Soldering takes place because of a bonding principle called
   A. cohesion
   B. adhesion
   C. flux
   D. abrasion

_____ 2. Soldering in which the solder melts below 800° F [427° C] is called
   A. brazing
   B. soft soldering
   C. hard soldering
   D. welding

_____ 3. Soldering in which the solder melts above 800° F [427° C] is called
   A. brazing
   B. soft soldering
   C. hard soldering
   D. A and C

_____ 4. Ordinary soft solder is an alloy of
   A. lead and tin
   B. lead and zinc
   C. tin and zinc
   D. lead, tin, and zinc

_____ 5. Safe solders for water pipes and food containers **do not** contain
   A. tin
   B. lead
   C. antimony
   D. silver

_____ 6. Pieces of solder that are pre-cut to a certain shape are called solder
   A. pre-forms
   B. forms
   C. shapes
   D. pre-cuts

_____ 7. Before soldering, the metal must be chemically cleaned with
   A. steel wool
   B. water
   C. flux
   D. abrasive cloth

_____ 8. A noncorrosive flux that should always be used when soldering electrical wiring is
   A. rosin
   B. zinc chloride
   C. sal ammoniac
   D. tallow

_____ 9. Cleaning and coating the faces of a soldering copper with solder is known as
   A. soldering
   B. leading
   C. tinning
   D. galvanizing

_____ 10. Connecting two pieces of metal together in several places with drops of solder is known as
   A. tacking
   B. spotting
   C. sweating
   D. fusing

(Continued on next page)

_____ 11. The most widely used hard solders are alloys of
  A. lead   C. silver
  B. tin   D. bronze

_____ 12. Most hard solders melt in what temperature range?
  A. 450-650° F [232-343° C]   C. 1100-1300° F [593-704° C]
  B. 850-1050° F [454-566° C]   D. 1400-1600° F [760-871° C]

_____ 13. A material that works well as a flux for hard soldering is
  A. rosin   C. sal ammoniac
  B. zinc chloride   D. borax

_____ 14. Brazing rods are made of what metal?
  A. bronze   C. silver
  B. brass   D. iron

_____ 15. At what temperature do most brazing rods melt?
  A. 1800° F [982° C]   C. 1300° F [704° C]
  B. 1600° F [871° C]   D. 800° F [427° C]

_____ 16. The method of brazing often used for mass production is
  A. torch brazing   C. silver brazing
  B. furnace brazing   D. bronze brazing

17-21. Short Answer. List five occupations that require an ability to solder.

17. _____

18. _____

19. _____

20. _____

21. _____

22-27. Short Answer. List six forms in which solder is made.

22. _____   25. _____

23. _____   26. _____

24. _____   27. _____

28-29. Short Answer. What two problems result when soldering coppers are overheated?

28. _____

29. _____

Name _____

Score _____

UNIT 28
Adhesive Bonding

1-7. Multiple Choice. Write the letter of the correct answer to each statement or question in the space at the left.

_____   1. Adhesive bonding means to join parts permanently
          A. by welding   C. with nonmetallic glues
          B. by soldering   D. all of the above

_____   2. Adhesives that soften when heated and harden when cooled are called
          A. thermoplastic   C. thermopliable
          B. thermosetting   D. thermosolids

_____   3. Adhesives that permanently harden with heat and pressure are called
          A. thermoplastic   C. thermopliable
          B. thermosetting   D. thermosolids

_____   4. Most structural adhesives for bonding metals are modified forms of which two kinds of plastics?
          A. phenolic and acrylic   C. nylon and silicone
          B. rubber and epoxy   D. epoxy and phenolic

_____   5. What test is used to check whether metal surfaces are clean enough to be adhesive-bonded?
          A. water adhesion test   C. visual inspection
          B. water-break test   D. wiping with a white cloth

_____   6. What kind of surface is preferred for adhesive bonding?
          A. smooth   B. rough

_____   7. How thick should the layer of adhesive be to obtain the strongest bonds?
          A. 0.001-0.003″ [0.025-0.08 mm]   C. 0.006-0.009″ [0.15-0.23 mm]
          B. 0.003-0.006″ [0.08-0.15 mm]   D. 0.009-0.012″ [0.23-0.30 mm]

8-13. Short Answer. List six advantages of adhesive bonding.

8. _____

9. _____

10. _____

11. _____

12. _____

13. _____

(Continued on next page)

14-16. Short Answer. List three disadvantages of adhesive bonding.

14. _____

15. _____

16. _____

17-20. Short Answer. Name four forces that may act alone or in combination to pull apart adhesive joints.

17. _____

18. _____

19. _____

20. _____

21-22. Short Answer. Two advantages of designing adhesive-bonded joints that interlock are

21. _____

22. _____

23-28. Short Answer. List six forms in which adhesives are available.

23. _____

24. _____

25. _____

26. _____

27. _____

28. _____

29-31. Short Answer. List three basic methods of testing the soundness of adhesive-bonded assemblies.

29. _____

30. _____

31. _____

UNIT 29

Sheet Metal Pattern Development, Hand Tools, and Cutting Tools

1-17. Multiple Choice. Write the letter of the correct answer to each statement or question in the space at the left.

_____   1. Sheet metal is metal that is no thicker than
              A. ⅛″ [3.2 mm]   C. ¼″ [6.35 mm]
              B. ³⁄₁₆″ [4.76 mm]   D. ⁵⁄₁₆″ [7.94 mm]

_____   2. A full-size drawing of the shape of the flat sheet needed to make a sheet metal object
              is called a
              A. stretchout   C. pattern
              B. sketch   D. A or C

_____   3. The kind of pattern development used to develop a cylinder or square box is called
              A. radial line   C. triangulation
              B. parallel line   D. formulation

_____   4. The kind of pattern development used to develop a cone is
              A. radial line   C. triangulation
              B. parallel line   D. formulation

_____   5. The kind of pattern development used to develop an object with an irregular shape
              is
              A. radial line   C. triangulation
              B. parallel line   D. formulation

_____   6. A fold along an edge of a sheet metal object that removes the sharp edge and makes
              a stronger edge is called a
              A. hem   C. joint
              B. seam   D. cuff

_____   7. Edges of sheet metal pieces that are fastened together to assemble parts of an object
              form a
              A. hem   C. joint
              B. seam   D. flange

_____   8. The gage now used to measure the thickness of iron and steel sheets is the
              A. United States Standard Gage   C. Manufacturer's Standard Gage
              B. National Iron and Steel Gage   D. American Standard Gage

(Continued on next page)

9. A tool used for scratching layout lines on sheet metal is
   A. the prick punch   C. the scriber
   B. the scratch awl   D. B and C

10. A hand tool used for making hems, seams, and other straight-line bends in thin sheet metal is the
    A. hand groover   C. hand bender
    B. hand seamer   D. hand former

11. A hand tool for finishing a standing grooved seam is the
    A. hand groover   C. hand bender
    B. hand seamer   D. hand former

12. What is the maximum thickness that should be cut with tin snips?
    A. 16 gage   C. 22 gage
    B. 20 gage   D. 24 gage

13. What feature of aviation snips makes it possible for them to cut metal with less effort than with tin snips?
    A. They have longer handles.   C. They are compound-levered.
    B. They have sharper blades.   D. They have serrated cutting edges.

14. What is the maximum thickness and kind of metal that is safe to cut with a squaring shear?
    A. 16-gage aluminum   C. 20-gage copper
    B. 16-gage mild steel   D. 20-gage mild steel

15. A hand-operated machine that cuts a 90-degree notch in sheet metal is called a
    A. squaring shear   C. notcher
    B. coper   D. squaring punch

16. A machine that is used to cut the discs needed for the covers or bottoms of round containers is called the
    A. disc shear   C. ring shear
    B. circle shear   D. ring and circle shear

17. A bench machine used for cutting small rods and for cutting heavier gage metals than can be safely cut on the squaring shear is the
    A. rod parter   C. lever shear
    B. bench shear   D. heavy-duty shear

(Continued on next page)

18-27. Matching. Match the hems and seams pictured with their names by writing the correct letters in the blanks at the left.

_____ 18. Lap seam

_____ 19. Standing seam

_____ 20. Standing grooved seam

_____ 21. Single hem

_____ 22. Cap strip seam

_____ 23. Outside corner lap seam

_____ 24. Wired edge

_____ 25. Pittsburgh lock seam

_____ 26. Double hem

_____ 27. Flush lap seam

28-30. Matching. Match the hammers pictured with their names by writing the correct letters in the blanks at the left.

_____ 28. Riveting hammer

_____ 29. Setting hammer

_____ 30. Raising hammer

31-34. Short Answer. Name four industries that employ skilled sheet metal workers.

31. _____

32. _____

33. _____

34. _____

(Continued on next page)

35-41. Short Answer. Name seven sheet metals that are commonly used.

35. _____

36. _____

37. _____

38. _____

39. _____

40. _____

41. _____

42-46. Short Answer. List five tools used to punch holes in sheet metal.

42. _____

43. _____

44. _____

45. _____

46. _____

47-48. Short Answer. Name two electrically powered tools used to speed the cutting of sheet metal.

47. _____

48. _____

Name _____

Score _____

UNIT 30
Bending Sheet Metal

1-10. Multiple Choice. Write the letter of the correct answer to each statement or question in the space to the left.

_____   1. The machine made especially for bending edges to use in hems and seams is the
      A. cornice brake   C. box and pan brake
      B. bar folder   D. press brake

_____   2. The machine made especially for folding all four sides of a one-piece pan or tray is the
      A. cornice brake   C. box and pan brake
      B. bar folder   D. press brake

_____   3. Stove pipes and other cylindrical shapes are formed from flat sheet metal on which machine?
      A. slip-roll forming machine   C. tube rolling machine
      B. turning machine   D. ring and circle former

_____   4. The machine used to form the rounded edge on the end of a cylinder for making a wired edge is the
      A. burring machine   C. setting-down machine
      B. wiring machine   D. turning machine

_____   5. The machine used to press the edge of the metal around a wire to finish a wired edge is the
      A. burring machine   C. setting-down machine
      B. wiring machine   D. turning machine

_____   6. The machine used to form the turned up edge on the end of a pipe or cylinder as the first step in making a single or double bottom seam is the
      A. burring machine   C. setting-down machine
      B. wiring machine   D. turning machine

_____   7. The machine used to close the flange of a round can bottom when making a single bottom seam is the
      A. double-seaming machine   C. crimping and beading machine
      B. setting-down machine   D. grooving machine

_____   8. The machine that turns a bottom seam against the side of a cylindrical container is the
      A. double-seaming machine   C. crimping and beading machine
      B. setting-down machine   D. grooving machine

(Continued on next page)

_____ 9. The machine that rolls a groove near the edge of a stove pipe to make it stronger is the
A. slip-roll forming machine   C. turning machine
B. crimping machine   D. beading machine

_____ 10. The wavy edge on one end of a stove pipe that makes it smaller so it will fit into another pipe the same size is made on a
A. slip-roll forming machine   C. turning machine
B. crimping machine   D. beading machine

11-17. Matching. Match the sheet metal stakes with their names by writing the correct letters in the blanks at the left.

_____ 11. Bevel-edge square stake

_____ 12. Blowhorn stake

_____ 13. Beakhorn stake

_____ 14. Hollow-mandrel stake

_____ 15. Hatchet stake

_____ 16. Double-seaming stake

_____ 17. Needle-case stake

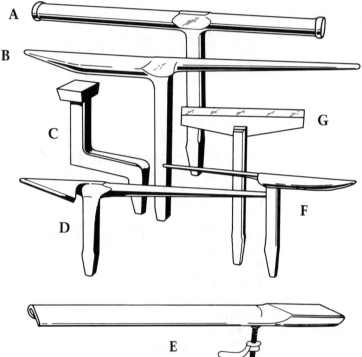

Name _____

Score _____

UNIT 31
Sheet Metal Manufacturing Methods

1-12. Multiple Choice. Write the letter of the correct response to each statement or question in the space at the left.

_____   1. The forming of one-piece containers using matched metal dies is called
A. shell punching   C. blanking
B. shell drawing   D. stretch forming

_____   2. A shallow forming operation used to make raised letters or decorative designs is called
A. coining   C. embossing
B. stretch forming   D. beading

_____   3. If the metal removed by the punch is scrap, then the operation is called
A. blanking   C. stamping
B. lancing   D. punching

_____   4. The process of cutting and expanding sheet metal by piercing it is called
A. blanking   C. stamping
B. lancing   D. punching

_____   5. A punch-and-die operation that removes only a small amount of metal for the purpose of making more accurately-sized pieces is called
A. shaving   C. lancing
B. scraping   D. coining

_____   6. A pressworking process used to make medals, coins, and parts with fine detail is called
A. embossing   C. beading
B. stretch forming   D. coining

_____   7. Forcing a drawn part through a highly polished tapered die is a process called
A. stretch forming   C. shell drawing
B. burnishing   D. coining

_____   8. The type of multiple station metal stamping die that cuts a finished part from a continuous strip of metal with each press stroke is called a
A. transfer die   C. stamping die
B. drawing die   D. progressive die

_____   9. The type of multiple station metal stamping die that cuts a finished part from a pre-cut blank with each press stroke is called a
A. drawing die   C. stamping die
B. transfer die   D. progressive die

(Continued on next page)

_____ 10. A process that uses successive sets of forming rolls to bend flat sheet metal into moldings, downspouts, gutters, and other shapes is called
A. roll forming
B. form rolling
C. metal spinning
D. shear spinning

_____ 11. Forming sheet metal into hollow cylindrical shapes by pressing the metal against a revolving chuck in a lathe is called
A. roll forming
B. form rolling
C. metal spinning
D. shear spinning

_____ 12. Forming thick metal discs into hollow cylindrical shapes by pressing the metal against a revolving chuck with a fully powered spinning tool is called
A. roll forming
B. form rolling
C. metal spinning
D. shear spinning

13-16. Short Answer. List the four headings under which sheet metal press-working operations are classified.

13. _____

14. _____

15. _____

16. _____

17-18. Short Answer. Name two shell-drawing processes that use rubber pads instead of a female die.

17. _____

18. _____

19-20. Short Answer. Name two types of explosive forming.

19. _____

20. _____

21-22. Short Answer.

_____ 21. A process similar to explosive forming but that uses a powerful electric spark as the energy source is called

_____ 22. The use of a powerful magnetic field to force metal to take the shape of a die is a process called

76

Name _Justin Stilwell_

Score _____

UNIT 32
Sand Casting

1-22. Multiple Choice. Write the letter of the correct answer to each statement or question in the space to the left.

_B_   1. A metal part made by pouring or forcing liquid metal into a mold is called a
    A. molding   C. pattern
    B. casting   D. forming

_C_   2. A factory that specializes in making metal castings is called a
    A. pattern shop   C. foundry
    B. casting factory   D. molding factory

_A_   3. A model made of wood, metal, wax, or plaster that is the size and shape needed to make a casting is called a
    A. pattern   C. model
    B. mold   D. duplicate

_B_   4. Patterns that are attached to wood or metal plates in order to speed up production of molds are called
    A. match-surface plates   C. production patterns
    B. match-plate patterns   D. manufacturing patterns

_B_   5. The taper on the sides of foundry patterns is called
    A. drift   C. slant
    B. draft   D. slope

_C_   6. Patterns must be made a little larger than the size of the finished casting to allow for
    A. shrinkage of the mold   C. shrinkage of the casting
    B. shrinkage of the pattern D. expansion of the mold

_D_   7. A special ruler used when making foundry patterns is called a
    A. pattern rule   C. stretch rule
    B. foundry rule   D. shrink rule

_B_   8. A hard sand form that is put into a mold to form a hole or hollow in a casting is called
    A. a dry-sand mold   C. an inclusion
    B. a core   D. an insert

_C_   9. A wooden or metal container for making sand molds is called a molding
    A. frame   C. flask
    B. box   D. case

(Continued on next page)

_A_ 10. The top half of the container used for making sand molds is called a
A. cope   C. top
B. drag   D. upper flask

_B_ 11. The bottom half of the container used for making sand molds is called the
A. cope   C. bottom
B. drag   D. bottom flask

_C_ 12. The line that separates the two halves of a flask is called the
A. dividing line   C. parting line
B. joining line   D. splitting line

_C_ 13. The screen used to sift out the lumps in sand and leave the sand fluffy is called a
A. sifter   C. riddle
B. sieve   D. grid

_D_ 14. A powdered material used to keep the sand from sticking to the pattern is called
A. mold release   C. molding compound
B. pattern compound   D. parting compound

_D_ 15. Holes made in a mold to allow steam and gases to escape are called mold
A. sprues   C. breathers
B. risers   D. vents

_B_ 16. The first part of the gating system which receives the liquid metal is called the
A. gate   C. runner
B. pouring basin   D. riser

_C_ 17. The hole through which the liquid metal flows into the mold cavity is the
A. gate   C. sprue
B. runner   D. riser

_D_ 18. The main ingredients in green sand are sand, water, and
A. flour   C. molasses
B. oil   D. clay

_A_ 19. Assuming the green sand has the right ingredients, mixing it with just enough water to make it stick together properly is called
A. tempering   C. mixing
B. hardening   D. milling

_C_ 20. A type of molding sand that uses oil instead of water to moisten it is called
A. dry sand   C. oil-bonded sand
B. oil sand   D. wet sand

_D_ 21. A casting process that uses patterns of polystyrene foam is called the
A. disposable pattern process   C. full-pattern process
B. plastic pattern process   D. full-mold process

_C_ 22. A mold made from sand and special foundry oils and baked until it is hard is called a
A. waterless sand mold   C. dry-sand mold
B. hard sand mold   D. oil-sand mold

Name *Justin Stilwell*

Score _____

UNIT 33
Investment Molding

1-8. Multiple Choice. Write the letter of the correct answer to each statement or question in the space to the left.

_A_   1. The kind of casting process that uses patterns of wax, plastic, or frozen mercury is known as
  A. investment molding   C. lost wax casting
  B. slush casting   D. both A and C

_D_   2. When several small wax patterns are attached to a central sprue, the arrangement is called a pattern
  A. cluster   C. stalk
  B. bush   D. tree

_A_   3. The kind of investment molding that uses a round steel container in which to make the mold is called
  A. investment flask molding   C. plaster molding
  B. investment shell molding   D. ceramic shell molding

_A_   4. The material used to make the mold for investment flask molding is
  A. plaster   C. sand
  B. ceramic   D. wax

_B_   5. Which kind of investment molding does not use a flask?
  A. investment flask molding   C. plaster molding
  B. investment shell molding   D. A and C

_B_   6. The materials used to make the mold for investment shell molding are
  A. plaster and ceramic sand   C. ceramic slurry and plaster
  B. ceramic slurry and ceramic sand D. sand and cement slurry

_B_   7. The wall thickness of investment shell molds is usually about how
  A. ⅛″ [3.2 mm]   C. ⅜″ [9.5 mm]
  B. ¼″ [6.35 mm]   D. ½″ [12.7 mm]

_B_   8. Investment molds must be heated before they are poured in order to
  A. dry the mold completely   C. make the casting as accurate as pos-
  B. melt the pattern   sible
                                 D. all of the above

9-10. Short Answer.

8 hrs.

9. For at least how many hours is an investment plaster mold allowed to air dry?

_300°F_

10. To what temperature is a ceramic shell mold heated in an oven?

Name _Austin Stilwell_

Score _____

UNIT 34
Permanent-Mold Casting and Die Casting

1-9. Multiple Choice. Write the letter of the correct answer to each statement or question in the space to the left.

_C_   1. Permanent mold casting uses molds made of
　　　　A. iron　　　　　　　　　　C. graphite
　　　　B. steel　　　　　　　　　　D. all of the above

_D_   2. Permanent mold castings can be made of
　　　　A. most nonferrous metals　　　C. some gray iron alloys
　　　　B. steel　　　　　　　　　　D. all of the above

_C_   3. The wall thickness of permanent mold castings is usually no thinner than
　　　　A. ⅛″ [3.2 mm]　　　　　　C. ¼″ [6.35 mm]
　　　　B. ³⁄₁₆″ [4.8 mm]　　　　　　D. ⅜″ [9.5 mm]

_C_   4. Permanent mold castings can be made to tolerances as small as plus or minus
　　　　A. 0.001″ [0.025 mm]　　　　C. 0.010″ [0.25 mm]
　　　　B. 0.005″ [0.13 mm]　　　　D. 0.020″ [0.51 mm]

_D_   5. In die casting, the liquid metal is
　　　　A. poured into the die　　　　C. forced into the die under low pressure
　　　　B. forced into the die with vacuum assistance　　　　D. forced into the die under high pressure

_C_   6. Die castings can be made as accurately as plus or minus
　　　　A. 0.002″ [0.05 mm]　　　　C. 0.006″ [0.15 mm]
　　　　B. 0.004″ [0.10 mm]　　　　D. 0.008″ [0.20 mm]

_B_   7. Die castings can be made with walls as thin as
　　　　A. ¹⁄₆₄″ [0.4 mm]　　　　　C. ¹⁄₁₆″ [1.6 mm]
　　　　B. ¹⁄₃₂″ [0.8 mm]　　　　　D. ⅛″ [3.2 mm]

_B_   8. Die-casting machines used for higher melting point metals, such as aluminum, are of a type known as
　　　　A. hot-chamber　　　　　　C. permanent-mold
　　　　B. cold-chamber　　　　　　D. pressure chamber

_A_   9. Die-casting machines usually used for low melting point metals, such as zinc alloys, are of a type known as
　　　　A. hot-chamber　　　　　　C. permanent-mold
　　　　B. cold-chamber　　　　　　D. vacuum

Name _Justin Stilwell_

Score _____

UNIT 35
Miscellaneous Casting Processes

1-9. Multiple Choice. Write the letter of the correct answer to each statement or question in the space to the left.

_B_ 1. Plaster mold casting is the same as investment flask molding except that
    A. molds are not heated
    B. patterns must have draft and are not lost
    C. castings are not as accurate
    D. castings are not as smooth

_A_ 2. A process that is used mostly for casting pipe, gun barrels, and other hollow objects is
    A. centrifugal casting
    B. semi-centrifugal casting
    C. centrifuge casting
    D. rotary casting

_B_ 3. A process used for casting solid objects in molds that are stacked so as to spin around the axis of the part being cast is known as
    A. centrifugal casting
    B. semi-centrifugal casting
    C. centrifuge casting
    D. rotary casting

_C_ 4. A kind of casting process that rotates molds placed in a circle around a central sprue is known as
    A. centrifugal casting
    B. semi-centrifugal casting
    C. centrifuge casting
    D. rotary casting

_B_ 5. A method of making hollow castings by pouring liquid metal into a metal mold and then quickly pouring it out is called
    A. coreless casting
    B. slush casting
    C. flood casting
    D. immersion casting

_C_ 6. Dipping a highly polished metal pattern into a pot of liquid metal to make hollow castings is called
    A. immersion casting
    B. submersion casting
    C. dip casting
    D. slush casting

_C_ 7. A molding method useful only for making small quantities of castings from low melting point metals is
    A. plaster mold casting
    B. slush casting
    C. silicone rubber molding
    D. dip casting

_C_ 8. Plaster for molds is made from
    A. plastic
    B. copper
    C. foundry plaster
    D. plaster of Paris

_A_ 9. If plaster is added to water rather than water to plaster, this minimizes
    A. air entrapment
    B. lumps
    C. early drying
    D. all of the above

Name _Justin Stilwell_

Score _____

UNIT 36
Melting and Pouring Metal

1-11. Multiple Choice. Write the letter of the correct answer to each statement or question in the space at the left.

_B_   1. A type of furnace that melts the metal in the same pot that it is poured from is called a
       A. pot furnace   C. electric arc furnace
       B. crucible furnace   D. cupola furnace

_C_   2. The types of furnaces used for melting large quantities of high melting point metals, such as iron, are the
       A. electric arc and crucible   C. electric arc, electric induction, and
       B. cupola and induction   cupola
                                      D. induction and crucible

_D_   3. Why must solid metal be completely dry before being added to a pot of liquid metal?
       A. Moisture will cool off the metal.   C. Moisture will combine with the
       B. Moisture will weaken the metal.   metal to form unwanted slag.
                                      D. Moisture can turn to steam and
                                      cause an explosion.

_C_   4. Crucibles can be prevented from sticking to the firebrick they rest on in the furnace by covering the firebrick with
       A. parting compound   C. corrugated cardboard
       B. brick dust   D. sand

_D_   5. The waste material containing oxides and other impurities that float on melted metal is called
       A. dross   C. slag
       B. sludge   D. A and C

_D_   6. Coarse-grained castings are usually the result of
       A. using too much flux   C. pouring the metal too cold
       B. using too little flux   D. pouring the metal too hot

_B_   7. The difference between the melting point of a metal and the temperature at which it is poured is called
       A. overheat   C. excess heat
       B. superheat   D. waste heat

_B_   8. The container used to transfer liquid metal from a furnace to the mold is called a
       A. dipper   C. bucket
       B. ladle   D. pot

Unit 36 (continued)

_C_

9. An instrument used to measure the temperature of liquid metal is called a
   A. thermometer   C. pyrometer
   B. meltometer   D. hygrometer

_D_

10. The process of removing castings from their molds by using vibrating conveyers or tables is called a
    A. shakedown operation   C. shakeup operation
    B. sorting out operation   D. shakeout operation

_C_

11. A finished casting is one that
    A. has had all the mold material cleaned off
    B. has had the sprue, gates, risers, and flash cut off
    C. has been cleaned and has had the sprue, gates, risers, and flash cut off
    D. has been cleaned, has had the sprue, gates, risers, and flash cut off, and has been machined if required

12-13. Short Answer. Protective clothing must be worn while pouring metal to guard against being burned from what two causes?

12. _Metal may be spilled from the ladle_

13. _Gas pockets in the mold and water in the ladle may cause an explosion_

14. Short Answer. Why is it necessary to carefully preheat some new furnace linings and new crucibles?

14. _To minimize the danger of cracking_

15-17. Short Answer. Name three ways castings are cleaned.

15. _SAND Blast_

16. _Shot Blast_

17. _tumbling_

(Continued on next page)

18-23. Short Answer. Look up the melting points of the following metals. Write the melting points in the blanks at the left.

787°F _____ 18. Zinc

1218°F _____ 19. Aluminum

1700°F _____ 20. Brass

1761°F _____ 21. Silver

2200°F _____ 22. Cast iron

2500°F _____ 23. Steel

24-33. Matching. The illustration has lettered elements. Write their names in the corresponding blanks.

24. (A) _CAP_

25. (B) _Face Shield_

26. (C) _leather apron_

27. (D) _long sleeves_

28. (E) _gauntlet gloves_

29. (F) _slag_

30. (G) _Slagging bar_

31. (H) _ladle_

32. (I) _high leather shoe_

33. (J) _mold_

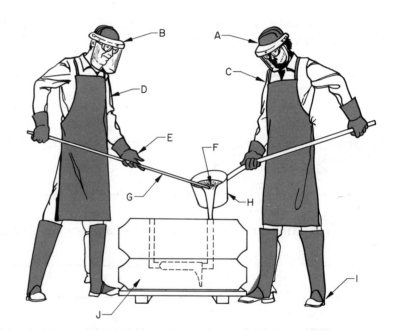

Name *Justin Stilwell*

Score _____

UNIT 37
Powder Metallurgy

1-8. Multiple Choice. Write the letter of the correct answer to each statement or question in the space to the left.

C   1. The process of making parts by compressing metal powders and then heating the parts in an oxygen-free furnace is known as
A. powder metal engineering   C. powder metallurgy
B. powder metal processing   D. powder metal technology

D   2. Powder metal parts that have been compressed but have not been heated in an oxygen-free furnace are called
A. stampings   C. forgings
B. green ware   D. green compacts

B   3. Heating powder metal parts in an oxygen-free furnace to bond the metal particles together is called
A. baking   C. roasting
B. sintering   D. firing

C   4. The powder metallurgy process **is not** economical for fewer than how many parts?
A. 100,000   C. 20,000
B. 50,000   D. 10,000

A   5. Most powder metal parts are
A. iron-base or copper-base   C. iron-base or nickel-base
B. aluminum-base or magnesium-base   D. copper-base or tungsten-base

D   6. The process of filling the pores of powder metal parts with oil is called
A. infiltration   C. pressure lubricating
B. absorption   D. impregnation

A   7. The process of sealing the pores of powder metal parts with a metal of lower melting point is called
A. infiltration   C. metal sealing
B. absorption   D. impregnation

A   8. What industry is the largest user of powder metal parts in the United States?
A. the automotive industry   C. the portable power tool industry
B. the small appliance industry   D. the jewelry industry

(Continued on next page)

9-12. Short Answer. List four metals that can be processed only by powder metallurgy.

9. _Copper / zinc_

10. _Copper / Tin_

11. _Iron / copper_

12. _Iron carbon / copper_

13-14. Short Answer. Name two important ways in which the powder metal process is unusual.

13. _Enables materials to be combined that were previously impossible_

14. _Parts of controlled density and porosity are made_

Name _Justin Stilwell_

Score _____

UNIT 38
Industrial Forging

1-9. Multiple Choice. Write the letter of the correct answer to each statement or question in the space to the left.

_C_   1. The process of hammering or pressing solid metal into the desired shape is called
A. stamping   C. forging
B. press working   D. extrusion

_B_   2. Forged parts are almost all made by
A. hand   C. a combination of hand and machine
B. machine   D. none of the above

_C_   3. A closed-die process for forging parts using steam hammers or board hammers is called
A. upset forging   C. drop forging
B. hammer or smith forging   D. press forging

_D_   4. A process that uses a slow squeezing action necessary for forging large objects is called
A. upset forging   C. drop forging
B. squeeze forging   D. press forging

_B_   5. A type of forging using steam- or air-powered presses having a flat anvil and hammer is known as
A. upset forging   C. drop forging
B. hammer or smith forging   D. press forging

_A_   6. A hot-forging method that increases the cross-sectional size of a bar is called
A. upset forging   C. drop forging
B. bulge forging   D. swaging

_D_   7. A cold-forging method that increases the cross-sectional size of a bar, as for making bolt heads, is called
A. cold upset forging   C. cold bulge forging
B. cold swaging   D. cold heading

_C_   8. A forging process that is used to reduce or taper the diameter or thickness of a bar is called
A. taper forging   C. roll forging
B. angle forging   D. swaging

(Continued on next page)

B   9. A process that is restricted to forging the ends of bars or tubes is known as
    A. end forging   C. upset forging
    B. swaging   D. cold heading

10-12. Short Answer. Name three advantages of hot forging.

10. _Forged parts are stronger than machined parts doesn't hurt the grain_

11. _Produces strong parts with complex more economically than machining_

12. _Little metal is lost in the process_

13-14. Short Answer. Name two disadvantages of hot forging.

13. _The hot temperatures cause rapid oxidation_

14. _Close tolerances can't be obtained due to scaling_

Name _Justin Stilwell_

Score _____

UNIT 39
Hand Forging

1-5. Matching. Match the parts of the anvil whown with the names by writing the correct letters in the blanks.

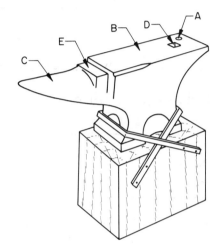

___C___ 1. Horn

___B___ 2. Face

___E___ 3. Cutting block

___D___ 4. Hardy hole

___A___ 5. Pritchel hole

6-9. Matching. Match the forging tools shown at the right with the names by writing the correct letters in the blanks.

___B___ 6. Heading tool

___A___ 7. Hand hammer

___D___ 8. Curved lip tongs

___C___ 9. Straight lip tongs

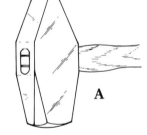

A

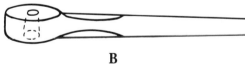

B

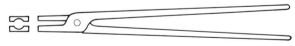

C

D

(Continued on next page)

10-12. Short Answer. Name three incandescent colors that indicate steel is hot enough to forge.

10. _bright red_

11. _orange_

12. _yellow_

13-18. Short Answer.

13. Why is it important that gas not be allowed to collect in a gas furnace before it is lighted?

Because it could result in an explosion.

14. When shutting off a gas furnace or forge, which should be turned off first, the gas or the air?

The gas should always be shut off first.

15. What causes steel to weaken when it is overheated?

Grain coarsening

16. What happens if metal is forged when it is too cold?

The metal can crack or split

17. A forge weld is made while the metal is heated to what color?

White

18. What is bulging the end of a bar by heating it and then ramming it against an anvil called?

upset

UNIT 40
Extrusion

1-7. Multiple Choice. Write the letter of the correct answer to each statement or question in the space to the left.

_C_   1. The process of shaping solid metal by forcing it through an opening in a die is called
　　A. intrusion 　　　　　　　　　　C. extrusion
　　B. protrusion 　　　　　　　　　 D. forging

_D_   2. Most hot extrusions are made on what kind of presses?
　　A. mechanically powered vertical 　　C. hydraulically powered vertical
　　　 presses 　　　　　　　　　　　　　 presses
　　B. mechanically powered horizontal 　D. hydraulically powered horizontal
　　　 presses 　　　　　　　　　　　　　 presses

_B_   3. What is the maximum possible length of extrusions on some machines?
　　A. 100 ft. 　　　　　　　　　　　C. 20 ft.
　　B. 50 ft. 　　　　　　　　　　　 D. 10 ft.

_D_   4. Hot aluminum extrusions may be as large in diameter as
　　A. 6″ [152 mm] 　　　　　　　　C. 18″ [457 mm]
　　B. 12″ [305 mm] 　　　　　　　 D. 24″ [610 mm]

_A_   5. Hot steel extrusions may be as large in diameter as
　　A. 6″ [152 mm] 　　　　　　　　C. 18″ [457 mm]
　　B. 12″ [305 mm] 　　　　　　　 D. 24″ [610 mm]

_B_   6. Cold extrusion is done with the metal
　　A. cooled below room temperature 　C. at room temperature or warmed a
　　B. at room temperature 　　　　　　　 few hundred degrees
　　　　　　　　　　　　　　　　　　 D. heated to 800° F [427° C]

_A_   7. A type of extrusion in which soft metal tubes are rapidly made from metal discs is
　　A. impact extrusion 　　　　　　C. punch extrusion
　　B. quick-draw extrusion 　　　　 D. squirt extrusion

8-10. Short Answer. List three advantages of hot extrusion.

8. _Lower pressure for forming_

9. _Able to make complex shapes_

10. _Able to produce larger parts._

(Continued on next page)

11. Short Answer. Explain the difference between forward and reverse extrusion.

11. In forward extrusion a ram pushes the metal into the die, and in reverse extrusion the ram pushes the die into the metal.

Name _Justin Stilwell_

Score _____

UNIT 41
Heat Treatment of Steel

1-27. Multiple Choice. Write the letter of the correct answer to each statement or question in the space to the left.

_D_   1. The process of changing the mechanical properties of metals by heating and cooling them while in a solid state is called
    A. metallurgy   C. tempering
    B. hardening   D. heat treating

_A_   2. The element in steel that determines whether or not it can be hardened is
    A. carbon   C. phosphorous
    B. silicon   D. sulfur

_A_   3. In order to harden steel by heat treatment, its carbon content must be higher than
    A. 0.30%   C. 0.60%
    B. 3.0%   D. 6.0%

_D_   4. The chemical combination of iron and carbon that occurs in unhardened steel at temperatures below 1330° F (721° C) is called
    A. iron carbide   C. cementite
    B. pearlite   D. both A and C

_B_   5. In unhardened steel, cementite is normally a mechanical mixture with
    A. austenite   C. pearlite
    B. ferrite   D. iron carbide

_D_   6. The name given to nearly pure iron is
    A. pearlite   C. cementite
    B. iron carbide   D. ferrite

_C_   7. Pearlite is the name given to a mixture of
    A. ferrite and pearlite   C. ferrite and cementite
    B. pearlite and cementite   D. ferrite and austenite

_C_   8. The amount of pearlite in unhardened steel increases as the carbon is increased to what percentage?
    A. 0.30%   C. 0.80%
    B. 0.60%   D. 1.50%

_B_   9. Steel with 0.80% carbon is called
    A. eutectic steel   C. austenitic steel
    B. eutectoid steel   D. ferritic steel

(Continued on next page)

_D_   10. When steel is heated to the correct hardening temperature, its internal structure should
   A. be all austenite
   B. have a coarse grain structure
   C. have a fine grain structure
   D. both A and C

_D_   11. The hardest and most brittle form of steel is known as
   A. ferrite
   B. austenite
   C. cementite
   D. martensite

_D_   12. The correct hardening temperature for steel is
   A. the upper critical temperature
   B. the lower critical temperature
   C. 50-100° F [10-38° C] above the lower critical temperature
   D. 50-100° F [10-38° C] above the upper critical temperature

_C_   13. The quenching solution that cools most rapidly is
   A. air
   B. water
   C. brine
   D. oil

_A_   14. Most plain-carbon steels are quenched in
   A. water or brine
   B. water or oil
   C. brine or oil
   D. air or brine

_B_   15. Most alloy steels are quenched in
   A. air or brine
   B. oil or air
   C. oil or water
   D. water or brine

_B_   16. Steel that has been hardened correctly
   A. will soften unless tempered
   B. may crack unless tempered immediately
   C. will crack if tempered immediately
   D. does not require tempering

_B_   17. A general rule for determining the length of time a steel part should be heated for tempering is
   A. two hours per inch [25.4 mm] of thickness
   B. one hour per inch [25.4 mm] of thickness
   C. one-half hour per inch [25.4 mm] of thickness
   D. one hour for each ¼" [6.35 mm] of thickness

_D_   18. After the part has reached the tempering temperature, it should be
   A. cooled in air
   B. cooled in water
   C. cooled slowly first to 400° F [204° C], then rapidly to room temperature
   D. either A or B

_D_   19. The heat-treatment process that is used to remove the most hardness from steel is
   A. normalizing
   B. process annealing
   C. spheroidizing annealing
   D. full annealing

_A_   20. Full annealing of steel requires it to be heated thoroughly at
   A. 50-100° F [10-38° C] above the upper critical temperature
   B. the upper critical temperature
   C. 1000-1300° F [538-704° C]
   D. 1300-1330° F [704-721° C]

Name Justin Stilwell

Unit 41 (continued)

_D_ 21. Full annealing requires that parts be cooled by
- A. very slow cooling in the furnace
- B. quenching in still air
- C. packing in lime or ashes
- D. A or C

_C_ 22. A kind of annealing used most for removing stresses from low-carbon steel is called
- A. normalizing
- B. spheroidizing annealing
- C. process annealing
- D. full annealing

_B_ 23. A kind of annealing used to make high-carbon steel more machinable is called
- A. normalizing
- B. spheroidizing annealing
- C. process annealing
- D. full annealing

_A_ 24. A heat-treating method used to relieve stresses in steel that requires heating well above the upper critical temperature followed by cooling in air is
- A. normalizing
- B. spheroidizing annealing
- C. process annealing
- D. full annealing

_C_ 25. The process that hardens a thin surface layer on low-carbon steel is called
- A. surface hardening
- B. skin hardening
- C. case-hardening
- D. shell hardening

_C_ 26. Low-carbon steel can absorb two elements that enable it to harden. These are
- A. carbon and oxygen
- B. nitrogen and hydrogen
- C. carbon and nitrogen
- D. nitrogen and oxygen

_B_ 27. Carburizing to a depth of $\frac{1}{16}$″ [1.6 mm] takes about how long?
- A. 24 hours
- B. 8 hours
- C. 1 hour
- D. 20 minutes

28. Short Answer. Accurate heat-treating furnace temperatures require the furnace to be equipped with

28. _Temperature-indcating control devices_

29-31. Short Answer. List three kinds of temperature-indicating materials available for indicating the temperature of heated steel.

29. _Pellets_

30. _Crayons_

31. _Paints_

(Continued on next page)

32-39. Short Answer. List eight properties of steel that can be changed by heat treatment.

32. Hardness
33. brittleness
34. toughness
35. tensile strength
36. ductility
37. malleability
38. machinability
39. elasticity

40-42. Short Answer. What tempering temperature is recommended for

540° 40. Screwdrivers

540° 41. Hammers

425° 42. Drills

43-45. Short Answer. List three carburizing methods used in case-hardening steel.

43. pack carburizing
44. gas carburizing
45. liquid carburizing

46. Short Answer. Name the nonpoisonous and noncombustible carburizing material recommended for school shop use.

46. Kasenit (a commercial carburizing compound)

47-50. Short Answer. Name four surface-hardening processes that do not add material to the surface of the steel being hardened.

47. Flame hardening
48. Induction hardening
49. laser hardening
50. electron beam hardening

UNIT 42
Abrasives

1-9. Multiple Choice. Write the letter of the correct answer to each statement or question in the space to the left.

_D_   1. The hardest natural abrasive is
     A. emery   C. crocus
     B. corundum   D. diamond

_D_   2. The hardest artificial abrasive is
     A. diamond   C. silicon carbide
     B. aluminum oxide   D. boron carbide

_B_   3. Artificial abrasives are harder than all the natural abrasives except
     A. crocus   C. emery
     B. diamond   D. corundum

_B_   4. The artificial abrasive best suited to grinding materials of high tensile strength is
     A. silicon carbide   C. boron carbide
     B. aluminum oxide   D. diamond

_B_   5. Most grinding wheels in use today are made with
     A. silicon carbide   C. boron carbide
     B. aluminum oxide   D. diamond

_A_   6. The artificial abrasive best suited for grinding materials of low tensile strength such as cast iron is
     A. silicon carbide   C. boron carbide
     B. aluminum oxide   D. diamond

_D_   7. The abrasive best suited to grinding space-age alloys and hardened high speed steels is
     A. diamond   C. boron nitride
     B. silicon carbide   D. cubic boron nitride

_D_   8. The abrasive best suited for grinding extremely hard materials such as carbide cutting tools is
     A. silicon carbide   C. boron carbide
     B. aluminum oxide   D. diamond

_C_   9. Removing small amounts of metal from hardened steel using a soft metal tool that is coated with a fine abrasive is called
     A. honing   C. lapping
     B. grinding   D. polishing

(Continued on next page)

10-14. Short Answer. List five common forms in which abrasives are used in metalworking.

10. _Abrasive cloth_

11. _loose grain and powder abrasive_

12. _abrasive compounds_

13. _grinding wheels_

14. _Sharpening stones_

15-17. Short Answer. What three properties should an abrasive have?

15. _hardness_

16. _fracture resistance_

17. _wear resistance_

18-20. Short Answer. Name three backing materials used in the manufacture of coated abrasives.

18. _Paper_

19. _cloth_

20. _fiber_

21-24. Short Answer.

21. How many holes are there in one square inch [25.4 mm] of a screen used for sizing 100-grain abrasive?

   100 holes

22. Why is it recommended that a drop of oil be used on the abrasive cloth for the final polishing of steel?

   To lower the amount of dust

23. What is the name for a pad of steel shavings used for cleaning and polishing metal?

   Steel wool

24. What can a worker wear when polishing or grinding to protect him- or herself against breathing abrasive dust?

   A respirator

Name _Justin Stilwell_

Score _____

UNIT 43
Grinding Wheels

1-11. Multiple Choice. Write the letter of the correct answer to each statement or question in the space to the left.

_____C_____ 1. Shaping metal by cutting with an abrasive wheel is known as
A. honing   C. grinding
B. lapping   D. polishing

_____D_____ 2. Small grinding wheels having a permanent shaft attached are called
A. mounted wheels   C. shaft wheels
B. attached wheels   D. arbor wheels

_____D_____ 3. The binding material that holds grains of abrasive together is called the
A. binder   C. glue
B. cement   D. bond

_____C_____ 4. Most grinding wheels are made with what kind of bond?
A. rubber   C. vitrified
B. shellac   D. resinoid

_____B_____ 5. Grinding wheels used for sharpening tools and knives have what kind of bond?
A. vitrified   C. shellac
B. silicate   D. rubber

_____C_____ 6. Grinding wheels used for finishing mill rolls and bearings have what kind of bond?
A. vitrified   C. shellac
B. silicate   D. rubber

_____A_____ 7. The property of a grinding wheel that refers to the tightness with which the abrasive grains are held in the wheel is called the
A. grade   C. composition
B. structure   D. hardness

_____B_____ 8. Softer grades of grinding wheels are used to grind materials that are
A. soft   B. hard

_____D_____ 9. The grade of a grinding wheel is determined by the
A. spacing of the abrasive grain   C. kind of bond used
B. hardness of the abrasive   D. amount of bond holding the grains

_____B_____ 10. The characteristic of a grinding wheel that refers to the amount of space between the abrasive grains is called the
A. grade   C. composition
B. structure   D. hardness

(Continued on next page)

_A_   11. Grinding wheels that cut most rapidly have a structure that is referred to as
A. open-grain   B. closed-grain

12-18. Short Answer. List seven factors that should be considered when selecting a grinding wheel for a job.

12. _Type of Grinding_

13. _The material_

14. _Amount of stock to be removed_

15. _Quality of finish_

16. _Area of wheel contact_

17. _wheel speed_

18. _Dry or wet grinding_

19-23. Short Answer. According to the standard marking system, what do the markings C60-E12V on a grinding wheel mean?

19. C _Abrasive type - Silicon type_

20. 60 _Grain size - 60-MED_

21. E _Grade - E_

22. 12 _Structure - 12 - OPEN_

23. V _Bond Type - vitrified_

24-29. Short Answer. In addition to the code number, which six other items of information should be given when ordering a grinding wheel?

24. _Shape_

25. _type_

26. _Diameter of wheel_

27. _width of wheel_

28. _diameter of hole_

29. _Speed_

30-31. Short Answer. Of what two materials are wheel cores for diamond grinding wheels made?

30. _Natural Diamonds_

31. _Artificial Diamonds_

100

Name _Justin Stilwell_

Score _____

UNIT 44
Utility Grinders

1-7. Multiple Choice. Write the letter of the correct answer to each statement or question in the space at the left.

___C___ 1. Grinders that are used for nonprecision grinding operations in which either the grinder or the work is hand-held are called
   A. nonprecision grinders
   B. hand grinders
   C. utility grinders
   D. off-hand grinders

___B___ 2. The grinding of burrs, sharp edges, flash, and other imperfections from castings is called
   A. off-hand grinding
   B. snagging
   C. trimming
   D. scarfing

___D___ 3. A utility grinder mounted on its own free-standing base is called
   A. a free-standing grinder
   B. an upright grinder
   C. a post grinder
   D. a pedestal grinder

___A___ 4. How close to the grinding wheel should the tool rest be placed?
   A. as close as possible
   B. ¹/₁₆″ [1.6 mm]
   C. ⅛″ [3.2 mm]
   D. ¼″ [6.35 mm]

___C___ 5. The main purpose of a grinding wheel guard is to
   A. limit grinding to a small part of the wheel
   B. protect the operator from flying sparks
   C. prevent pieces from being thrown from a broken grinding wheel
   D. prevent the workpiece from being pulled into the grinding wheel

___D___ 6. For best eye protection when grinding, always
   A. use the grinder's glass eye shield
   B. use the grinder's glass eye shield and wear goggles
   C. use the grinder's glass eye shield and wear a face shield
   D. either B or C

___A___ 7. The large metal washers that should be used on both sides of a grinding wheel are called
   A. safety washers
   B. discs
   C. flanges
   D. rings

(Continued on next page)

8-9. Short Answer.

8. How should you check for cracks before mounting a new grinding wheel?

   Strike wheel lightly with a light object a good wheel will ring clearly

9. Between what surface speeds are grinding wheels usually run?

   4000 - 6500 FPM

10-13. Short Answer. List four kinds of grinding operations that utility grinders are used for.

10. _Prep weld joints_
11. _Sharpen tools_
12. _Smooth welds_
13. _remove burrs_

14-17. Short Answer. List four types of utility grinders.

14. _Bench_
15. _Pedestal_
16. _Wet_
17. _Portable_

18-19. Short Answer. Give two benefits of wet grinding.

18. _Carries away heat_
19. _Washes away bits of metal_

20. Short Answer. Why is it that grinder shafts have left-hand threads on the left-hand end of the shaft and right-hand threads on the right-hand end?

20. _In order so the nuts will tighten as the shaft turns._

Name _Justin Stihwell_

Score _____

UNIT 45
Sharpening Tools by Hand Grinding

1-8. Multiple Choice. Write the letter of the correct answer to each statement or question in the space to the left.

_A_   1. A grinding wheel that has become clogged by grinding soft materials is said to be
     A. loaded   C. plugged
     B. glazed   D. clogged

_B_   2. A grinding wheel that has a shiny cutting surface due to dull abrasive grains is said to be
     A. loaded   C. slick
     B. glazed   D. smooth

_C_   3. Removing the dull grains of abrasive from a grinding wheel is called
     A. sharpening   C. dressing
     B. truing   D. re-shaping

_B_   4. Re-shaping a grinding wheel to its proper shape and removing any high spots is called
     A. sharpening   C. dressing
     B. truing   D. re-shaping

_C_   5. High-speed steel tools that are overheated by grinding and then dipped in cold water may be damaged by
     A. excessive hardening   C. cracking
     B. loss of hardness   D. loss of carbon

_C_   6. A plain-carbon steel cutting tool will lose some of its hardness if it gets so hot from grinding that it turns
     A. yellow or brown   C. purple or blue
     B. brown or purple   D. blue or gray

_D_   7. Sharpening a tool on the face of a grinding wheel makes a cutting edge that is called
     A. curved   C. face-ground
     B. circle-ground   D. hollow-ground

_C_   8. Sharpening the cutting edge of a tool with a small oilstone is called
     A. stoning   C. honing
     B. lapping   D. dressing

(Continued on next page)

9-12. Short Answer. Give four reasons why it is important to use sharp cutting tools.

9. _It is safer_

10. _leaves better finish on part_

11. _requires less cutting force_

12. _Performs in a expected way_

13-15. Short Answer.

13. Why should soft metals such as lead, copper, and aluminum not be ground on a grinding wheel?

Soft metals will load the wheel

14. Why should only the face of a grinding wheel be used for grinding?

It will thin the wheel causing it to break

15. What tool can be used for measuring cutting edge angles if a gage is not available?

A protractor

Name _Justin Stilwell_

Score _____

UNIT 46
Metal Finishing

1-16. Multiple Choice. Write the letter of the correct answer to each statement or question in the space to the left.

_B_   1. Before applying paint or enamel to a metal surface, it should be degreased with
    A. alcohol   C. lacquer thinner
    B. mineral spirits   D. detergent

_C_   2. Before applying lacquer to a metal surface, it should be degreased with
    A. alcohol   C. lacquer thinner
    B. mineral spirits   D. detergent

_D_   3. Removing metal oxidation by dipping in an acid solution is called
    A. degreasing   C. priming
    B. dissolving   D. pickling

_B_   4. Chromate and phosphate coatings are used to improve which metal property?
    A. heat resistance   C. electrical resistance
    B. corrosion resistance   D. electrical conduction

_C_   5. Black oxide coatings are a type of
    A. enamel coating   C. chemical conversion coating
    B. electroplated coating   D. lacquer coating

_D_   6. A paint that is used as a first coat because it sticks well to bare metal is called
    A. an undercoat   C. a filler
    B. a green coat   D. a primer

_B_   7. A special paint used as a first coat on galvanized steel is
    A. zinc oxide   C. zinc chloride
    B. zinc chromate   D. red lead

_A_   8. A liquid coating that is colorless when it dries is
    A. lacquer   C. enamel
    B. paint   D. none of the above

_B_   9. Colors formed on some metals simply by heating them are called
    A. thermocolors   C. chemical colors
    B. oxide colors   D. thermal colors

_C_   10. Coating an object with a thin layer of metal by electro-deposition is known as
    A. electrocoating   C. electroplating
    B. electroforming   D. electrofinishing

(Continued on next page)

_B_ 11. Making an object entirely by electro-deposition is known as
A. electrocoating
B. electroforming
C. electroplating
D. electrofinishing

_D_ 12. An electrochemical finishing method commonly used on aluminum and magnesium to improve corrosion resistance, surface hardness, and electrical resistance is known as
A. alodizing
B. calorizing
C. cladding
D. anodizing

_C_ 13. Bonding a thin layer of corrosion-resistant metal to another by rolling two sheets together under high pressure is called
A. mechanical plating
B. electroless plating
C. cladding
D. pressure plating

_D_ 14. A hard glass-like coating applied to metal by spraying and then baking at high temperature is called
A. porcelain enamel
B. baked enamel
C. ceramic enamel
D. both A and C

_A_ 15. Making a finish smooth and bright by rubbing it with hard, smooth tools is called
A. burnishing
B. polishing
C. peening
D. planishing

_C_ 16. Using a wood dowel, oil, and abrasive flour to make round, polished spots on a metal surface is called
A. burnishing
B. spin finishing
C. spot finishing
D. dowel finishing

17-22. Short Answer. Name six reasons for finishing metal.

17. _Protects it from corrading_

18. _wear longer_

19. _makes it stable_

20. _Improves value_

21. _Improves appearance_

22. _Neutralizes the chemical reaction_

23-26. Short Answer. Name four ways of applying paints, enamel, or lacquer to metal.

23. _brushing_

24. _dipping_

25. _Spraying_

26. _Powder Coating_

Name Justin Stihell

Unit 46 (continued)

27-34. Short Answer. List eight metals that are commonly electroplated onto other metals.

27. Aluminum

28. Lead

29. Tin

30. Cadmium

31. chromium

32. copper

33. Zinc

34. nickel

Name _Justin Stilwell_

Score _____

UNIT 47
Buffing

1-5. Multiple Choice. Write the letter of the correct answer to each statement or question in the space to the left.

_B_   1. Polishing metal to a smooth, bright finish using a soft revolving wheel to which an abrasive has been applied is called
A. brushing   C. rotary polishing
B. buffing   D. grinding

_C_   2. How much buffing compound should be put on the wheel?
A. a heavy layer   C. a little at a time
B. a moderate amount   D. none

_A_   3. The metal being polished should contact the buffing wheel
A. near the bottom   C. on the front near the top
B. on the front in the middle   D. it should not contact it

_B_   4. The actual work of polishing the metal in buffing is done by the
A. buffing wheel   C. pressure of the metal against the
B. buffing compound   wheel
                                 D. heat generated by rubbing the wheel

_D_   5. Buffing compound should be removed from the workpiece by washing with
A. hot water and mild soap   C. hot water and washing soda
B. a solvent such as mineral spirits   D. either A or C

6-9. Short Answer. Name four materials used in making buffing wheels and tell what each is used for.

6. ___Wire - Cleaning / burnishing___

7. ___leather/felt - coarse buffing compounds for rough surfaces___

8. ___Cotton muslin - Intermediate buffing___

9. ___Cotton flannel - fine buffing___

10-11. Short Answer. Name two ways that fiber bristle and wire wheels are used in metal finishing.

10. ___Satin finish___

11. ___Clean / burnishing___

Unit 47 (continued)

12-13. Short Answer. Name two ways that abrasive flap and abrasive impregnated nylon wheels are used in metal finishing.

12. _Deburring_

13. _Fast Smoothing of rough Surfaces_

14-19. Short Answer. Name six abrasives used in making buffing compounds.

14. _Tripoli_

15. _Crocus_

16. _Lime_

17. _rouge_

18. _emery_

19. _aluminum oxide_

20-22. Short Answer.

20. What device should be worn to protect against breathing too much dust when buffing?
    A respirator

21. What is the cause of work coming from the buffing wheel greasy and dirty?
    To much buffing Compound on wheel

22. How is buffing done when thousands of identical parts require it?
    With an automatic buffing machine

Name _Justin Stilwell_

Score _____

UNIT 48
Metal Marking Systems

1-7. Multiple Choice. Write the letter of the correct response to each statement or question in the space provided at the left.

_D_ 1. Metal marking with the use of hardened steel dies is called
- A. etching
- B. printing
- C. engraving
- D. stamping

_B_ 2. Marking or decorating metal by using acid to eat away the unwanted metal is known as
- A. chemical engraving
- B. chemical etching
- C. mechanical etching
- D. electrochemical etching

_C_ 3. A marking system that dissolves away the unwanted metal by passing an electric current through an electrolyte-moistened stencil in contact with the workpiece is called
- A. chemical milling
- B. electrical etching
- C. electrochemical etching
- D. electromechanical etching

_A_ 4. Using an electric arc to mark metals is called
- A. mechanical etching
- B. electrical etching
- C. electronic etching
- D. electromechanical etching

_C_ 5. Marking metal with the use of vibrating or revolving metal cutting tools is known as
- A. mechanical etching
- B. incising
- C. engraving
- D. hobbing

_A_ 6. The high-technology machining process that is also an efficient process for engraving metals of any hardness is
- A. laser machining
- B. electrical discharge machining
- C. electron beam machining
- D. ultrasonic machining

_D_ 7. Marking metal by forcing ink through openings in a thin piece of metal or cardboard is known as
- A. printing
- B. lithography
- C. silk screening
- D. stenciling

8-10. Short Answer. List three common uses for metal marking systems.

8. ___Serial numbers___

9. ___the size & type of tool___

10. ___trade marks___

UNIT 49
Holding Workpieces for Machining

1-5. Multiple Choice. Write the letter of the correct response to each statement or question in the space to the left.

_____ 1. Getting a workpiece correctly positioned and clamped in preparation for machining is called
   A. setting up   C. setting up work
   B. setup work   D. all of the above

_____ 2. Bolts made especially for fitting into the T-slots of machine tables are called
   A. machine bolts   C. T-slot bolts
   B. machine table bolts   D. workpiece bolts

_____ 3. A device used in production work for quickly clamping a workpiece for machining, but which has no provision for guiding tools is called a
   A. jig   C. rig
   B. fixture   D. nest

_____ 4. A device used in production work for holding a workpiece and which has provision for guiding the cutting tool is called a
   A. jig   C. rig
   B. fixture   D. nest

_____ 5. A removable drill bushing that allows a larger tool to be used at the same location after drilling is called a
   A. flanged bushing   C. slip bushing
   B. flush bushing   D. removable bushing

6-10. Short Answer. List five possible results of a workpiece springing or moving while it is being machined.

6. _____

7. _____

8. _____

9. _____

10. _____

(Continued on next page)

11-20. Matching. Match the setup tools pictured with their names by writing the correct letters in the blanks.

_____ 11. Finger clamp

_____ 12. Parallels

_____ 13. T-slot bolt

_____ 14. Plain clamp

_____ 15. Parallel clamp

_____ 16. Jackscrew

_____ 17. U-clamp

_____ 18. Step block

_____ 19. Screw-heel clamp

_____ 20. Goose-neck clamp

A

B

C

D

E

F

G

H

I

J

UNIT 50
Lubricants and Cutting Fluids

1-13. Multiple Choice. Write the letter of the correct response to each statement or question in the space to the left.

_____   1. Machine oil, used for lubricating machinery, is obtained from
            A. animals   C. petroleum
            B. vegetables   D. minerals

_____   2. The stiffness or thickness of lubricating oils is called
            A. fluidity   C. pour rate
            B. viscosity   D. weight

_____   3. Some lathe spindles require a thin lubricating oil called
            A. machine oil   C. spindle oil
            B. cylinder oil   D. way oil

_____   4. An oil that **is not** recommended for lubricating machine tools is
            A. mineral oil   C. vegetable oil
            B. animal oil   D. motor oil

_____   5. Glycerin is a lubricant obtained from
            A. animal fats   C. petroleum
            B. alcohol   D. either A or B

_____   6. A vegetable oil sometimes used in racing car engines is
            A. linseed oil   C. castor oil
            B. sunflower seed oil   D. soybean oil

_____   7. Greases are made from
            A. animal and vegetable fats   C. vegetable fats and petroleum
            B. animal fats and petroleum   D. petroleum and alcohol

_____   8. Greases are classified according to stiffness on a scale of
            A. 0 (softest) to 6   C. 0 (softest) to 100
            B. 0 (stiffest) to 6   D. 0 (stiffest) to 100

_____   9. A black, slippery form of carbon used as a lubricant is called
            A. lamp black   C. carbon black
            B. carbonite   D. graphite

_____ 10. The white powder mixed with linseed oil to make a good high-pressure lubricant is
             a compound of
             A. titanium   C. lead
             B. magnesium   D. zinc

(Continued on next page)

_____ 11. Cutting fluids made of chemical compounds in a water solution, and which generally **do not** contain petroleum products, are called
   A. chemical cutting fluids   C. water-soluble oils
   B. soluble oils   D. coolants

_____ 12. Because of the fire hazard, water-based cutting fluids **should not** be used when machining
   A. cast iron   C. manganese
   B. aluminum   D. magnesium

_____ 13. Most machining operations can be done without a cutting fluid on which metal because of its natural graphite lubrication?
   A. cast iron   C. magnesium
   B. aluminum   D. brass

14-16. Short Answer. List three advantages of using greases instead of oil.

14. _____

15. _____

16. _____

17-20. Short Answer. List four methods used to deliver oil to machine lubrication points.

17. _____

18. _____

19. _____

20. _____

21-24. Short Answer. List four advantages of using cutting fluids.

21. _____

22. _____

23. _____

24. _____

25-28. Short Answer. List four ways of applying cutting fluids to cutting tools.

25. _____

26 _____

_____

_____

Name _____

Score _____

UNIT 51
Stock Cutoff Machines

1-13. Multiple Choice. Write the letter of the correct response to each statement or question in the space at the left.

_____   1. A device used on cutoff saws that enables the operator to cut several pieces of the same length without having to measure each piece is called a
    A. cutoff gage   C. stock support
    B. stock stop   D. length meter

_____   2. Depending on the make and type of power hacksaw, the number of cutting strokes per minute may range between
    A. 15 and 130   C. 35 and 150
    B. 25 and 140   D. 45 and 180

_____   3. How many strokes per minute should be used for wet-cutting low-carbon steel?
    A. 120-150   C. 60-90
    B. 90-120   D. 40-60

_____   4. Power hacksaw blades for cutting thin-walled tubing, angles, and stock less than ¼″ [6.4 mm] thick should have what tooth pitch?
    A. 18 teeth per inch [1.4 mm pitch]   C. 6 teeth per inch [4 mm pitch]
    B. 10 teeth per inch [2.5 mm pitch]   D. 14 teeth per inch [1.8 mm pitch]

_____   5. In order to prevent stripping of hacksaw teeth, a minimum of how many teeth should contact the workpiece at all times?
    A. 1   C. 3
    B. 2   D. 4

_____   6. Power hacksaw blades for cutting bars from ¼″ [6.4 mm] to ¾″ [19 mm] thick should have what tooth pitch?
    A. 18 teeth per inch [1.4 mm pitch]   C. 6 teeth per inch [4 mm pitch]
    B. 10 teeth per inch [2.5 mm pitch]   D. 14 teeth per inch [1.8 mm pitch]

_____   7. Power hacksaw blades for cutting bars from about 1″ [25 mm] to 2″ [50 mm] thick should have what tooth pitch?
    A. 14 teeth per inch [1.8 mm pitch]   C. 6 teeth per inch [4 mm pitch]
    B. 10 teeth per inch [2.5 mm pitch]   D. 4 teeth per inch [6.4 mm pitch]

_____   8. Band-saw blades made of what material are preferred for cutoff work?
    A. carbon tool steel   C. high-speed steel
    B. alloy tool steel   D. tungsten carbide

(Continued on next page)

9. To withstand high cutting pressures, band-saw blades for cutoff work are usually at least how wide?
   A. ½" [13 mm]   C. 1" [25 mm]
   B. ¾" [19 mm]   D. 1¼" [32 mm]

10. For cutting material up to 1" [25 mm] thick, what band-saw tooth form is recommended?
    A. regular   C. skip
    B. hook   D. tungsten carbide

11. For cutting material thicker than 1" [25 mm], what band-saw tooth form is recommended?
    A. regular   C. skip
    B. hook   D. tungsten carbide

12. A type of stock cutoff saw that uses a low-rpm circular saw blade is called a
    A. cold saw   C. circular saw
    B. buzz saw   D. disc saw

13. Abrasive cutoff saws are most useful for cutting
    A. mild steel   C. thin-walled tubing
    B. soft nonferrous metals   D. very tough or hardened metals

Name _____

Score _____

UNIT 52
Band Sawing and Machining

1-10. Multiple Choice. Write the letter of the correct response to each statement or question in the space at the left.

_____ 1. Because of its ability to make curved cuts, a vertical band saw is also called a
   A. jig saw   C. universal saw
   B. contouring machine   D. profile saw

_____ 2. Making parts completely on a band saw is known as
   A. band machining   C. band fabrication
   B. band manufacturing   D. band construction

_____ 3. Two operations other than sawing commonly done on vertical band saws are
   A. filing and nibbling   C. filing and polishing
   B. polishing and notching   D. notching and nibbling

_____ 4. Which type of band-saw drive system requires that speed changes be made only when the machine is running?
   A. cone-pulley drive   C. cog-belt drive
   B. all-gear drive   D. variable-speed drive

_____ 5. What is the recommended band-saw cutting speed for dry-cutting of aluminum between ½" [13 mm] and 1" [25 mm] thick?
   A. 125 fpm [38 mpm]   C. 500 fpm [152 mpm]
   B. 250 fpm [76 mpm]   D. 800 fpm [244 mpm]

_____ 6. What is the recommended band saw cutting speed for dry-cutting of low-carbon steel between ½" [13 mm] and 1" [25 mm] thick?
   A. 125 fpm [38 mpm]   C. 500 fpm [152 mpm]
   B. 250 fpm [76 mpm]   D. 800 fpm [244 mpm]

_____ 7. What type of band-saw blade tooth set is recommended for most cutting on vertical band saws?
   A. raker   C. alternate
   B. wavy   D. any of the above

_____ 8. What type of band-saw blade tooth form is recommended for most cutting?
   A. skip tooth   C. hook
   B. regular   D. tungsten carbide

(Continued on next page)

_____ 9. What is the minimum radius of a curved cut that can be made with a ⅜" [9.5 mm] wide blade?
     A. 3¾" [95 mm]   C. 1¼" [32 mm]
     B. 2½" [64 mm]   D. ⅝" [16 mm]

_____ 10. What pitch band-saw blade is recommended for cutting metal ½" [13 mm] to 2" [50 mm] thick?
     A. 18 teeth per inch [1.4 mm pitch]   C. 10 teeth per inch [2.5 mm pitch]
     B. 14 teeth per inch [1.8 mm pitch]   D. 8 teeth per inch [3.2 mm pitch]

UNIT 53
Drilling Machines

1-9. Multiple Choice. Write the letter of the correct response to each statement or question in the space at the left.

_____ 1. A large powerful drill press that has a single fixed spindle with an automatic feed is called a
    A. sensitive drill press   C. upright drill press
    B. turret drill press   D. radial drill press

_____ 2. A type of drilling machine that has two or more drill presses mounted on a common base is called a
    A. multiple-spindle drill press   C. turret drill press
    B. gang-drill press   D. radial drill press

_____ 3. A type of drill press that has several spindles that all revolve and advance at the same time, enabling several holes to be drilled at the same time, is called a
    A. multiple-spindle drill press   C. turret drill press
    B. gang-drill press   D. upright drill press

_____ 4. A type of drill press that has a single spindle mounted on a movable arm that can swing around its supporting post or column is called a
    A. universal drill press   C. upright drill press
    B. movable drill press   D. radial drill press

_____ 5. A type of drill press that has several spindles that revolve around a common point, but which allows only one tool at a time to be in the operating position, is called a
    A. multiple-spindle drill press   C. turret drill press
    B. gang-drill press   D. sensitive drill press

_____ 6. The part of the drill press that revolves and also carries the drilling tool is called the
    A. spindle   C. collar
    B. quill   D. drill holder

_____ 7. The part of the drill press that causes the drilling tool to move up and down is called the
    A. spindle   C. collar
    B. quill   D. column

_____ 8. A 16″ [406 mm] upright drill press
    A. can drill a hole in the center of a 16″ [406 mm] diameter circle
    B. can drill a hole in the center of a 32″ [812 mm] diameter circle
    C. has a table 16″ [406 mm] square
    D. has a table that can be raised or lowered 16″ [406 mm]

(Continued on next page)

_____ 9. An 8′ [2438 mm] radial drill press
  A. can drill a hole in the center of an 8′ [2438 mm] circle
  B. can drill a hole in the center of a 16′ [4876 mm] circle
  C. has a column 8′ [2438 mm] high
  D. has an arm that measures 8′ [2438 mm] from the center of its column to its tip

10-20. Matching. Match the parts in the illustration with their names by writing the correct letters in the blanks.

_____ 10. On-off switch

_____ 11. Spindle

_____ 12. Table

_____ 13. Column

_____ 14. Base

_____ 15. Feed handle

_____ 16. Quill

_____ 17. Table lock

_____ 18. Table positioning handle

_____ 19. Speed control handle

_____ 20. T-slot

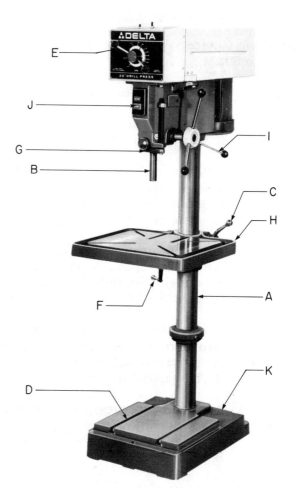

UNIT 54
Drills, Sleeves, Sockets, and Chucks

1-10. Multiple Choice. Write the letter of the correct response to each statement or question in the space at the left.

_____ 1. The type of drill most often used in metalwork is the
    A. spade drill   C. straight-fluted drill
    B. twist drill   D. core drill

_____ 2. The type of drill that is used for drilling out cored holes in castings is the
    A. oil-hole twist drill   C. twist drill
    B. core drill   D. cast hold drill

_____ 3. The type of drill that is used for drilling very deep holes is called a
    A. spade drill   C. gun drill
    B. twist drill   D. core drill

_____ 4. The type of drill that has replaceable blades is the
    A. spade drill   C. straight-fluted drill
    B. twist drill   D. core drill

_____ 5. Drills that use replaceable carbide inserts for cutting edges are called
    A. spade drills   C. carbide-tipped drills
    B. insert drills   D. carbide drills

_____ 6. Most drilling in metal is done with drills made of
    A. carbon steel   C. solid tungsten carbide
    B. tungsten carbide tipped steel   D. high-speed steel

_____ 7. Drills used for drilling very hard or abrasive materials have cutting edges made of
    A. tungsten carbide   C. carbon steel
    B. high-speed steel   D. any of the above

_____ 8. The kind of taper used on taper-shanked drills is the
    A. Jarno   C. Morse
    B. Brown and Sharpe   D. ¼″ per foot [20.8 mm/m]

_____ 9. A drill with a small taper shank size can be made to fit a drill-press spindle with a larger taper shank size by using a drill
    A. socket   C. collar
    B. sleeve   D. spacer

(Continued on next page)

_____ 10. A drill with a taper shank size larger than will fit into a drill-press spindle can be made to fit by using a drill
A. socket
B. sleeve
C. collar
D. spacer

11-14. Short Answer. Drills are made according to four standard size systems. Name them.

11. _____

12. _____

13. _____

14. _____

15-25. Matching. Match the parts of the drills shown with their names by writing the correct letters in the blanks.

_____ 15. Point

_____ 16. Shank

_____ 17. Tang

_____ 18. Neck

_____ 19. Body

_____ 20. Web

_____ 21. Cutting edge

_____ 22. Margin

_____ 23. Flute

_____ 24. Body clearance

_____ 25. Heel

CROSS-SECTION VIEWS OF WEB

BOTTOM VIEW OF POINT

UNIT 55
Drilling

1-9. Multiple Choice. Write the letter of the correct response to each statement or question in the space at the left.

_____ 1. When small drills are run at too slow an rpm, it
A. reduces drill wear
B. increases drill wear
C. decreases drill breakage
D. increases drill breakage

_____ 2. The correct rpm to run a ½″ [12.7 mm] drill for a cutting speed of 200 fpm [60.96 mpm] is
A. 1600
B. 400
C. 1528
D. A or C

_____ 3. If the corners of drill cutting edges wear away quickly, the
A. rpm should be increased
B. rpm should be reduced
C. feed rate should be increased
D. feed rate should be reduced

_____ 4. The tool used to remove a tapered-shank drill from a drill-press spindle is called a drill
A. drift
B. draft
C. wedge
D. wrench

_____ 5. The kind of drill used to make a starting hole for other drills is called a
A. combination drill and countersink
B. center drill
C. starting drill
D. A and B

_____ 6. A small hole drilled through a workpiece to make it easier for a large drill to cut is called a
A. relief hole
B. center hole
C. starting hole
D. pilot hole

_____ 7. To prevent a hand-fed twist drill from acting like a corkscrew when it breaks through the bottom of a workpiece, use a
A. very slow feed rate
B. normal feed rate
C. very fast feed rate
D. slower rpm

_____ 8. Drilling with one or more smaller size drills that leave only a small amount of metal for the final drill to remove is called
A. stage drilling
B. step drilling
C. progressive drilling
D. pilot drilling

_____ 9. The distance a drill would travel in one minute if it were laid on its side and rolled determines its
A. feed rate
B. cutting speed
C. shank size
D. need for cutting fluid

UNIT 56
Other Drill-Press Operations

1-5. Matching. Match the reamers pictured with their names by writing the correct letters in the blanks.

_____ 1. Taper hand reamer

_____ 2. Straight-fluted hand reamer

_____ 3. Straight shank reamer

_____ 4. Adjustable hand reamer

_____ 5. Expansion hand reamer

A

B

C

D

E

6-16. Multiple Choice. Write the letter of the correct response to each statement or question in the space at the left.

_____ 6. When you machine-ream holes less than ½″ [12.7 mm] in diameter, how much smaller than the reamer size should they be drilled?
    A. 0.002″ [0.05 mm]   C. ¹⁄₆₄″ [0.4 mm]
    B. 0.005″ [0.13 mm]   D. ¹⁄₃₂″ [0.8 mm]

_____ 7. When you machine-ream holes ½″ [12.7 mm] and larger in diameter, they should be drilled how much smaller than the reamer size?
    A. 0.002″ [0.05 mm]   C. ¹⁄₆₄″ [0.4 mm]
    B. 0.005 ″ [0.013 mm]   D. ¹⁄₃₂″ [0.8 mm]

_____ 8. The maximum cut size recommended for hand reamers is
    A. 0.002″ [0.05 mm]   C. ¹⁄₆₄″ [0.4 mm]
    B. 0.005″ [0.13 mm]   D. ¹⁄₃₂″ [0.8 mm]

_____ 9. Cutting speeds for machine reaming should be
    A. the same as for drilling   C. ½ to ⅔ of the speed used for drilling
    B. ½ to ⅔ faster than for drilling   D. ⅓ to ½ of the speed used for drilling

_____ 10. Feed rates for machine reaming should be
    A. the same as for drilling   C. faster than for drilling
    B. slower than for drilling   D. none of the above

_____ 11. The standard countersink angle for flat-head screws is
    A. 60 degrees   C. 90 degrees
    B. 82 degrees   D. 110 degrees

_____ 12. A tool used to enlarge the top of a hole for a cap screw is called a
    A. combination drill and countersink   C. counterbore
    B. countersink   D. reamer

_____ 13. A drill-press operation that removes just enough metal from around the top of a hole to make a flat, smooth bearing surface is called
    A. spot finishing   C. spot countersinking
    B. spot counterboring   D. spot facing

_____ 14. The tapping attachment that **does not** require the drill-press spindle to be reversed in order to back out the tap is the
    A. nonreversing type   C. automatic type
    B. reversing type   D. universal type

_____ 15. The type of tap that should be used in a tapping attachment is the
    A. gun tap   C. helical or spiral-fluted tap
    B. hand tap   D. A or C

_____ 16. Using a revolving single-point cutting tool to enlarge a drilled hole is known as
    A. gun drilling   C. boring
    B. rough reaming   D. finish reaming

Name _____

Score _____

UNIT 57
Drill Sharpening

1-4. Multiple Choice. Write the letter of the correct response to each statement or question in the space at the left.

_____ 1. The correct lip clearance angle for drilling most steel is
      A. 4-8 degrees   C. 8-12 degrees
      B. 6-10 degrees   D. 10-14 degrees

_____ 2. The standard included angle for twist drills is
      A. 59 degrees   C. 118 degrees
      B. 90 degrees   D. 135 degrees

_____ 3. The rake angle formed when the angle of the drill flutes is greater than 90 degrees makes a
      A. positive rake   C. negative rake
      B. zero or neutral rake   D. reverse rake

_____ 4. To safely drill free-machining brass and some types of plastics, the drill point should be modified to provide a
      A. positive rake   C. negative rake
      B. zero or neutral rake   D. B or C

5-7. Short Answer. List three drill point measurements that must be correct in order for a twist drill to cut properly.

5. _____

6. _____

7. _____

8-10. Short Answer. What three things must be watched when sharpening a drill?

8. _____

9. _____

10. _____

Name _____

Score _____

UNIT 58
The Metalworking Lathe

1-20. Matching. Match each lathe part with its name by writing the correct letters in the blanks.

_____   1. Bed

_____   2. Bed ways

_____   3. Headstock

_____   4. Tailstock

_____   5. Tool post

_____   6. Apron

_____   7. Compound rest

_____   8. Saddle

_____   9. Lead screw

_____   10. Gear box

_____   11. Feed reverse lever

_____   12. Speed change levers

_____   13. Spindle nose

_____   14. Half nut lever

_____   15. Power feed clutch

_____   16. Friction-clutch control

_____   17. Carriage hand-wheel

_____   18. Feed rod

_____   19. Rack

_____   20. Tailstock spindle clamp

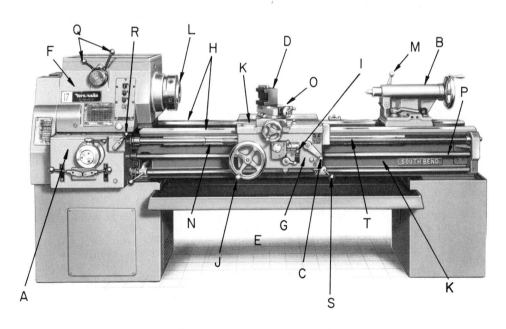

(Continued on next page)

21-26. Multiple Choice. Write the letter of the correct response to each statement or question in the space at the left.

_____ 21. The type of lathe used for production runs of a few hundred parts is the
A. manually operated screw machine
B. manually operated turret lathe
C. numerically controlled turret lathe
D. all of the above

_____ 22. The type of lathe used for production runs of thousands of identical parts is the
A. manually operated turret lathe
B. numerically controlled turret lathe
C. automatic lathe
D. vertical turret lathe

_____ 23. The size of a horizontal lathe is measured by the
A. maximum diameter and maximum length of stock it can turn
B. maximum diameter of stock it can turn and the length of its bed
C. maximum diameter of stock it can turn and the maximum horsepower available for cutting
D. maximum diameter of stock it can turn, maximum length of stock it can turn, and maximum horsepower

_____ 24. The purpose of back gears on a lathe is to
A. provide a faster range of spindle speeds
B. provide a slower range of spindle speeds
C. provide power to the gearbox
D. change the feed direction to the lead screw

_____ 25. Power feed for turning and facing is controlled by using the
A. carriage hand-wheel and cross-feed knob
B. friction clutch and apron feed-change lever
C. half-nut lever
D. all of the above

_____ 26. The feed rate for power longitudinal or cross feeding is changed by shifting the position of the
A. spindle speed-change levers
B. back-gear lever
C. quick-change gearbox levers
D. feed-change lever

UNIT 59
Methods of Holding Workpieces in a Lathe

1-3. Matching. Match each type of spindle nose pictured with its name by writing the correct letters in the blanks.

_____ 1. Cam-lock spindle nose

_____ 2. Threaded spindle nose

_____ 3. Long-taper key-drive spindle nose

A   B   C

4-8. Matching. Match each type of lathe chuck pictured with its name by writing the correct letters in the blanks.

_____ 4. Independent chuck

_____ 5. Universal chuck

_____ 6. Collet chuck

_____ 7. Spindle chuck

_____ 8. Step chuck

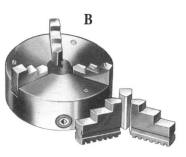

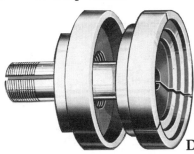

A   B   C   D   E

(Continued on next page)

9-16. Matching. Match each lathe accessory or centering aid pictured with its name by writing the correct letters in the blanks.

_____ 9. Faceplate

_____ 10. Wiggler or center finder

_____ 11. Dial indicator

_____ 12. Lathe dog

_____ 13. Live tailstock center

_____ 14. Lathe mandrel

_____ 15. Steady rest

_____ 16. Follower rest

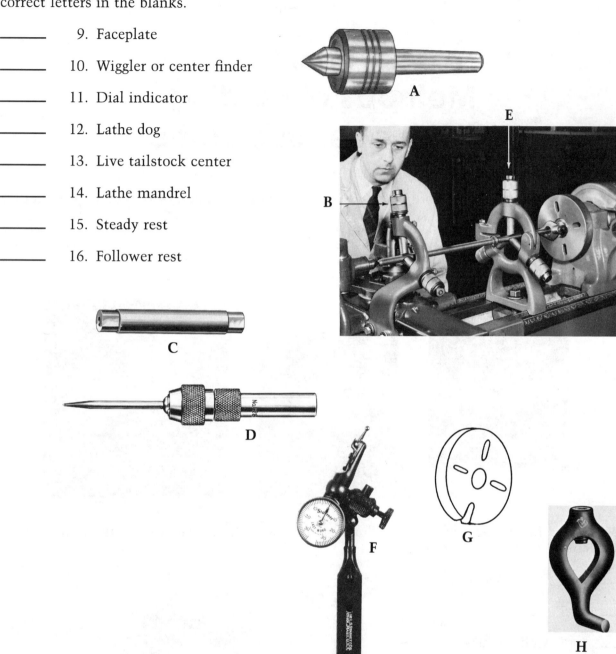

UNIT 60
Lathe Cutting Tools, Toolholders, Cutting Speeds, and Feed Selection

1-13. Matching. Match the cutting tool terms with the labeled parts of the cutting tool pictured by writing the correct letters in the blanks.

_____   1. Flank

_____   2. Heel

_____   3. Shank

_____   4. Cutting edge

_____   5. Nose radius

_____   6. Face

_____   7. Nose angle

_____   8. End-relief angle

_____   9. Side-rake angle

_____   10. Side-relief anglc

_____   11. Back-rake angle

_____   12. Side cutting-edge angle

_____   13. End cutting-edge angle

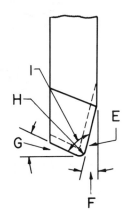

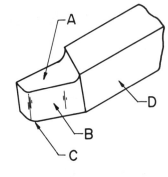

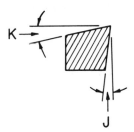

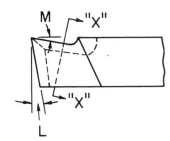

(Continued on next page)

14-22. Matching. Match each of the toolholders pictured with its name by writing the correct letters in the blanks.

_____ 14. 16½-degree straight turning

_____ 15. Knurling

_____ 16. Boring

_____ 17. Right-hand turning

_____ 18. Threading

_____ 19. Straight cutoff

_____ 20. Left-hand turning

_____ 21. Zero-degree straight turning

_____ 22. Throwaway insert

23-30. Multiple Choice. Write the letter of the correct response to each statement or question in the space to the left.

_____ 23. Most lathe cutting tools used in schools are made of
  A. high-carbon steel
  B. high-speed steel
  C. cast alloys
  D. cemented carbide

_____ 24. Cast alloy cutting tools are made of
  A. alloy steel
  B. cemented carbide
  C. cobalt alloyed with other nonferrous metals
  D. ceramic

_____ 25. Most lathe cutting tools used in production work are made of
  A. cast alloy
  B. ceramic
  C. high-speed steel
  D. cemented carbide

_____ 26. Ceramic cutting tools
  A. can be used only as throwaway inserts
  B. are made chiefly of aluminum oxide
  C. can cut hardened steels without using cutting fluids
  D. all of the above

_____ 27. The hardest of the metal-cutting tool materials is
  A. coated cemented carbide
  B. diamond
  C. ceramic
  D. cast alloy

_____ 28. Carbide grades C-1 through C-3 are recommended for cutting
    A. only cast iron
    B. steel and steel alloys
    C. cast iron and nonferrous metals
    D. steel and nonferrous metals

_____ 29. Carbide grades C-4 through C-8 are recommended for cutting
    A. cast iron and nonferrous metals
    B. steel and steel alloys
    C. cast iron, steel, and steel alloys
    D. only nonferrous metals

_____ 30. Longer-wearing carbide cutting tools have been made possible by
    A. improved heat treatment methods
    B. forming them of smaller powder metal particles
    C. using higher sintering temperatures in their manufacture
    D. the addition of very thin coatings of one or more very hard materials

31-33. Short Answer. Calculate the answers to the following problems:

_____ 31. At what rpm should a ⅜″ [9.5 mm] diameter tool steel workpiece run for a cutting speed of 90 fpm [27.4 mpm]?

_____ 32. At what rpm should a 1½″ [38.1 mm] diameter aluminum workpiece run for a cutting speed of 200 fpm [61 mpm]?

_____ 33. At what rpm should a 6″ [152.4 mm] diameter cast iron workpiece run for a cutting speed of 60 fpm [18.29 mpm]?

Name _____

Score _____

UNIT 61
Sharpening Lathe Cutting Tools

1-8. Multiple Choice. Write the letter of the correct response to each statement or question in the space at the left.

_____   1. High-speed steel and cast alloy cutting tools should be sharpened on grinding wheels made of
  A. emery   C. aluminum oxide
  B. silicon carbide   D. diamond

_____   2. Carbide-tipped cutting tools must be sharpened on grinding wheels made of
  A. special silicon carbide   C. diamond
  B. aluminum oxide   D. A or C

_____   3. The two cutting tool shapes most often used for lathework are
  A. right-hand turning tool and left-hand   C. right-hand turning tool and right-hand facing tool
     facing tool
  B. left-hand turning tool and right-hand   D. left-hand turning tool and left-hand facing tool
     facing tool

_____   4. To reduce the tendency of radius tools to chatter, they should have
  A. no back-rake   C. less end-relief than turning tools
  B. less side-relief than turning tools   D. all of the above

_____   5. Cutoff tool blades should never be sharpened on the
  A. top   C. front
  B. side   D. A and C

_____   6. To provide a cleaner cutoff than a blade with a square end, the cutoff tool should be ground
  A. to a point at its center   C. with a side-rake sloping to the right
  B. with a side-rake sloping to the left   D. at an angle across its end, making a point on the right side

_____   7. Threading tools for 60-degree threads should have
  A. no back-rake   C. no side-rake
  B. 5 degrees of back-rake   D. 5 degrees of side-relief

_____   8. Formed threading tools should only be sharpened on the
  A. left side   C. end
  B. right side   D. top

Unit 61 (continued)

9-12. Short Answer. Place the following tool grinding steps in their correct order by numbering them from 1-4.

———————————————   9. Grind the side-rake angle.

———————————————   10. Grind the end cutting-edge angle and end-relief angle.

———————————————   11. Grind the side cutting-edge angle and the side-relief angle.

———————————————   12. Grind the nose radius.

Name _____

Score _____

UNIT 62
Drilling, Reaming, Countersinking, and Counterboring in a Lathe

1-9. Multiple Choice. Write the letter of the correct response to each statement or question in the space at the left.

_____ 1. Center-drilling to provide a starting hole for other drills, or to make a bearing surface for lathe centers, is done with a
   A. countersink
   B. counterbore
   C. combination drill and countersink
   D. combination drill and counterbore

_____ 2. During center-drilling, if the tailstock is not lined up with the headstock, the result may be
   A. a hole drilled off-center
   B. an egg-shaped center hole
   C. a broken center drill
   D. a bent center drill

_____ 3. The marks on the rear of the tail-stock that indicate whether the tailstock centerline is lined up with the headstock centerline are called
   A. setover marks
   B. alignment marks
   C. realignment marks
   D. centerline marks

_____ 4. What kind of toolholder is used to hold straight-shank drilling tools in the tailstock?
   A. none
   B. a collet chuck
   C. a drill chuck
   D. a special straight-shank adapter

_____ 5. Cutting speeds for reamers, countersinks, and counterbores should be how fast in relation to cutting speeds for drilling?
   A. the same
   B. ¼ to ½ as fast
   C. 2 to 3 times faster
   D. ½ to ⅔ as fast

_____ 6. What should always be the first step in drilling a hole in solid metal held in a lathe?
   A. center-drilling
   B. counterboring
   C. filing
   D. none of the above

_____ 7. All straight-shank drilling tools are held in a drill chuck mounted in the
   A. headstock
   B. tailstock

_____ 8. Tailstock alignment can be corrected using
   A. a drill chuck
   B. varying the speed
   C. setover screws
   D. all of the above

_____ 9. When drilling steel, keep the center drill lubricated with
   A. cutting oil
   B. ionized water
   C. liquid carbon
   D. white lead

Name _____

Score _____

UNIT 63
Straight Turning, Facing, and Boring

1-10. Multiple Choice. Write the letter of the correct response to each statement or question in the space to the left.

_____   1. For turning, the point of the lathe cutting tool may be set between
A. exact center and 5 degrees above center
B. exact center and 5 degrees below center
C. 5 degrees below center and 5 degrees above center
D. exact center and 10 degrees above center

_____   2. The kind of lathe turning tool that has its cutting edge on the left side is called a
A. left-hand turning tool
B. right-hand turning tool

_____   3. The recommended angle between the cutting edge of the lathe tool and the side of the workpiece is
A. 45 degrees
B. 60 degrees
C. 80 degrees
D. 90 degrees

_____   4. To prevent the lathe tool from cutting more deeply into the workpiece than desired, never set it at an angle greater than
A. 45 degrees
B. 60 degrees
C. 80 degrees
D. 90 degrees

_____   5. Whenever possible, the direction of lathe turning should be towards the
A. headstock
B. tailstock

_____   6. For facing cuts the point of the tool should be set
A. exactly on center
B. 5 degrees above center
C. 5 degrees below center
D. 10 degrees above center

_____   7. For heavy facing cuts that start at the outside and cut towards center, which kind of facing tool should be used?
A. right-hand facing tool
B. left-hand facing tool

_____   8. Using a single-point cutting tool to machine the inside of a hole is called
A. internal machining
B. inside machining
C. broaching
D. boring

_____   9. The first cut, from which other measurements start, is called the
A. initial cut
B. facing
C. reference cut
D. turning cut

_____   10. Cutting across the end of a workpiece is called
A. boring
B. straight turning
C. facing
D. finish cutting

Name _____

Score _____

UNIT 64
Taper Turning

1-5. Multiple Choice. Write the letter of the correct response to each statement or question in the space at the left.

_____ 1. Which taper-turning method is best for turning short, steep tapers?
   A. tailstock offset   C. taper attachment
   B. compound rest   D. all of the above

_____ 2. Which method of taper turning is best for turning long, shallow tapers?
   A. tailstock offset   C. taper attachment
   B. compound rest   D. A and C

_____ 3. At what angle, measured from the lathe centerline, should the compound rest be set for turning a 60-degree point on a punch?
   A. 30 degrees   C. 90 degrees
   B. 60 degrees   D. 120 degrees

_____ 4. What is the name of the screws used to offset the tailstock for cutting a taper?
   A. offset screws   C. tailstock adjustment screws
   B. alignment screws   D. setover screws

_____ 5. The amount of tailstock offset can be measured by
   A. measuring the offset of the tailstock   C. using a dial indicator placed against
      alignment marks   the tailstock spindle
   B. measuring the offset of the headstock   D. all of the above
      and tailstock centers

6-7. Short Answer. Calculate the answers to the following problems:

_____ 6. Calculate the angle to set the compound rest for turning the taper on the part shown.

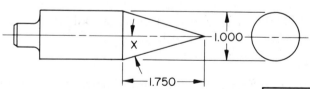

Inch	mm
1.000	25.4
1.750	44.45

_____   7. Calculate the amount of tailstock setover needed for turning
the taper on the part shown.

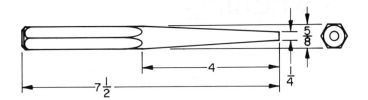

Inch	mm
¼	6.35
⅝	15.88
4	101.60
7½	190.50

8-10. Short Answer. What three things must be considered before choosing a taper-turning method?

8. _____

9. _____

10. _____

Name _____

Score _____

UNIT 65
Knurling

1-2. Multiple Choice. Write the letter of the correct response to each statement in the space at the left.

_____ 1. Pressing a tool with grooved hardened steel rolls into the surface of a revolving workpiece in the lathe is called
A. curling
B. knurling
C. roll forming
D. roll forging

_____ 2. Knurling should be done using a
A. slow rpm and a feed rate of about .005″ to .015″ [.13 to .38 mm]
B. high rpm and a feed rate of about .005″ to .015″ [.13 to .38 mm]
C. slow rpm and a feed rate of about 0.020″ to 0.0335″ [0.50 to 0.89 mm]
D. high rpm and a feed rate of about 0.020″ to 0.0335″ [0.50 to 0.89 mm]

3-4. Short Answer. Name two kinds of knurling patterns.

3. _____

4. _____

5-7. Short Answer. Name three sizes of knurling patterns that are available.

5. _____

6. _____

7. _____

8-10. Short Answer. List three reasons why knurling is done.

8. _____

9. _____

10. _____

Name _____

Score _____

UNIT 66
Filing and Polishing

1-8. Multiple Choice. Write the letter of the correct response to each statement or question in the space at the left.

_____ 1. Compared to turning, filing in a lathe is done at what rpm?
  A. twice as slow
  B. the same speed
  C. twice as fast
  D. four times as fast

_____ 2. What kind of file is used for lathe filing?
  A. double-cut hand file
  B. single-cut mill file
  C. long-angle lathe file
  D. either B or C

_____ 3. Compared to turning, abrasive polishing in the lathe is done at what rpm?
  A. twice as fast
  B. three times as fast
  C. about the same
  D. A or B

_____ 4. Abrasive polishing in the lathe can produce a bright mirror finish on
  A. tough metals like bronze
  B. soft metals like aluminum and brass
  C. hard metals like steel
  D. all metals

_____ 5. Adding a few drops of oil to the abrasive is recommended when polishing
  A. cast iron
  B. steel
  C. soft metals like aluminum
  D. all metals

_____ 6. Filing work while it is revolving in the lathe is done primarily to
  A. remove sharp edges
  B. add a decorative pattern
  C. polish it
  D. make facing cuts

_____ 7. Ordinary single-cut mill files also work well for lathe filing.
  A. yes
  B. no

_____ 8. How long should a file used for lathe filing be?
  A. 5-6 inches
  B. 7-9 inches
  C. 8-10 inches
  D. 12 inches

9-10. Short Answer. On what two things does the kind of abrasive and grit size used for polishing depend?

9. _____

10. _____

Name _____

Score _____

UNIT 67
Cutting Threads on the Lathe

1-8. Multiple Choice. Write the letter of the correct answer to each statement or question in the space at the left.

_____ 1. The point of the threading tool should be set
    A. exactly on the workpiece centerline
    B. between zero and 5 degrees above center
    C. between zero and 5 degrees below center
    D. none of the above

_____ 2. The tool used to set a 60-degree threading tool square with the workpiece is the
    A. center gage
    B. center head
    C. try square
    D. V-block

_____ 3. When cutting a 60-degree right-hand thread, the compound rest should be set at an angle of
    A. 14½ degrees to the right
    B. 14½ degrees to the left
    C. 29 degrees to the right
    D. 29 degrees to the left

_____ 4. When cutting a 60-degree thread, the tool is fed into the work for each successive cut with the
    A. cross-slide
    B. compound rest

_____ 5. For cutting a left-hand thread,
    A. the tool bit is reversed
    B. the lead screw direction is reversed
    C. the spindle rotation is reversed
    D. the apron feed selector is reversed

_____ 6. For cutting an even number of threads per inch, which lines on the thread dial may be used?
    A. any even-numbered line
    B. any odd-numbered line
    C. any numbered line
    D. any line

_____ 7. Which lines on the thread dial may be used for cutting an odd number of threads per inch?
    A. any even-numbered line
    B. any odd-numbered line
    C. any numbered line
    D. any line

_____ 8. A cutting oil should be used when cutting threads in a workpiece made of
    A. aluminum
    B. brass
    C. cast iron
    D. steel

9-10. Short Answer. Name the two kinds of thread-cutting tools used for cutting threads on a lathe.

  9. _____

10. _____

UNIT 68
Milling Machines

1-8. Multiple Choice. Write the letter of the correct response to each statement or question in the space to the left.

_____ 1. The type of milling machine used most for mass-production manufacturing is the
A. bed type
B. column-and-knee type
C. planer type
D. special-purpose type

_____ 2. The type of milling machine that has a work-holding table that can be moved in all three directions is the
A. bed type
B. column-and-knee type
C. planer type
D. all of the above

_____ 3. A universal milling machine differs from a plain milling machine in what way?
A. The table can be pivoted on its longitudinal axis.
B. The table can be swiveled in a horizontal plane.
C. The knee can be swiveled on its vertical axis.
D. The knee can be pivoted on its transverse axis.

_____ 4. It is best to set the depth of cut on a vertical column-and-knee milling machine by
A. lowering the vertical spindle
B. raising the knee
C. blocking up the workpiece with parallels
D. all of the above

_____ 5. Precise movement of the milling table in all directions is normally provided by
A. precision measuring rods and micrometers
B. vernier scales and magnifiers
C. a micrometer collar attached to each feed screw
D. gage blocks

_____ 6. End-milling operations may be performed on
A. vertical milling machines
B. horizontal milling machines
C. universal milling machines
D. all of the above

_____ 7. Movement of the milling machine table from side to side is called
A. transverse movement
B. longitudinal movement
C. vertical movement
D. lateral movement

_____ 8. Which method of milling may damage the cutter or workpiece on machines without anti-backlash devices?
A. up milling
B. down milling

(Continued on next page)

9-10. Matching. Match the milling methods pictured with their names by writing the correct letters in the blanks.

_____ 9. Down milling

_____ 10. Up milling

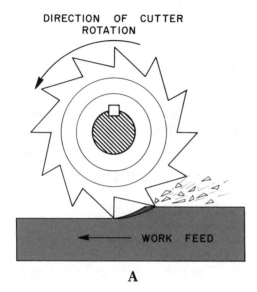

A

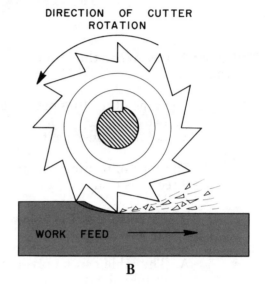

B

UNIT 69
Workpiece-Holding Devices and Accessories

1-3. Matching. Match each type of milling vise with its name by writing the correct letters in the blanks.

_____ 1. Plain vise

_____ 2. Swivel vise

_____ 3. Universal vise

4-7. Matching. Match each of the milling accessories with its name by writing the correct letters in the blanks.

_____ 4. Dividing head

_____ 5. Vertical milling attachment

_____ 6. Universal spiral milling attachment

_____ 7. Circular milling attachment

B

C

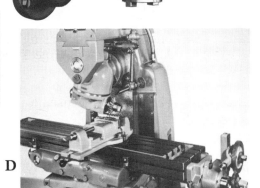
D

(Continued on next page)

8-15. Matching. Match each of the tool-holding accessories with its name by writing the correct letters in the blanks.

_____ 8. Style-A arbor

_____ 9. Style-B arbor

_____ 10. Style-C arbor

_____ 11. Arbor adapter

_____ 12. Collet adapter

_____ 13. Straight-shank end-mill holder

_____ 14. Boring head

_____ 15. Quick-change tool-holding system

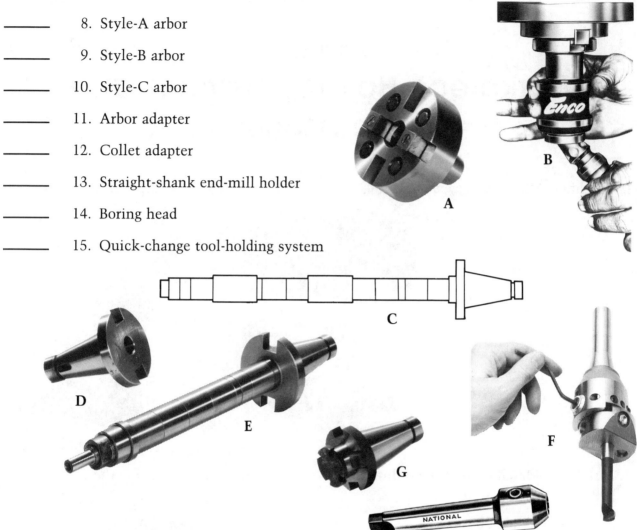

16-18. Multiple Choice. Write the letter of the correct response to each statement or question in the space at the left.

_____ 16. The steep self-releasing taper being used on most milling machine arbors is the
A. Brown and Sharpe Taper   C. national milling machine taper
B. Morse Taper   D. Jarno Taper

_____ 17. The style arbor used for light-duty milling operations on horizontal milling machines is
A. style A   B. style B

_____ 18. The style arbor used for holding shell end-milling cutters is
A. style A   C. style C
B. style B   D. all of the above

UNIT 70
Milling Cutters

1-11. Matching. Match the milling cutters with their names by writing the correct letters in the blanks.

_____   1. Plain

_____   2. Plain side

_____   3. Half-side

_____   4. Staggered-tooth side

_____   5. Slitting saw

_____   6. Single-angle

_____   7. Double-angle

_____   8. Convex

_____   9. Corner-rounding

_____   10. Concave

_____   11. Spur gear

A

B

C

D

E

F

G

H

I

J

K

(Continued on next page)

12-21. Matching. Match the end milling cutters with their names by writing the correct letters in the blanks.

_____ 12. Four-flute double-end

_____ 13. Two-flute double-end

_____ 14. Four-flute single-end straight-shank

_____ 15. Two-flute ball-end

_____ 16. Four-flute taper-shank

_____ 17. Carbide-tipped four-flute single-end straight-shank

_____ 18. Shell end mill

_____ 19. T-slot cutter

_____ 20. Woodruff key-seat cutter

_____ 21. Two-flute single-end

A

B

C

D

E

F

G

H

I

J

22-26. Multiple Choice. Write the letter of the correct response to each statement or question in the space at the left.

_____ 22. The type of cutter best suited for use on light-duty milling machines found in schools is the
A. inserted-tooth
B. solid high-speed steel
C. solid carbide
D. carbide-tipped

_____ 23. The type of end mill that can plunge-cut like a drill is the
A. shell end mill
B. multiple-flute end mill
C. ball end mill
D. carbide-insert end mill

_____ 24. Rigid vibration-free machines are required in order to use milling cutters made
A. of carbon steel
B. of high-speed steel
C. of cast alloy
D. with tungsten carbide tips

_____ 25. Very large cutters are often made
A. of solid carbon steel
B. of solid high-speed steel
C. with inserted teeth of cutting tool material
D. of solid carbide

_____ 26. Looking at the spindle nose, which way must a right-hand cutter rotate in order to cut?
A. clockwise
B. counterclockwise

UNIT 71
Cutting Speeds and Feeds for Milling

1-3. Multiple Choice. Write the letter of the correct response to each statement or question in the space at the left.

_____ 1. The cutting speed of a milling cutter is the distance a point on the cutting edge travels in one
   A. revolution
   B. second
   C. minute
   D. hour

_____ 2. Recommended cutting speeds for different metals are obtained by
   A. consulting a table of cutting speeds
   B. consulting the machine's rpm chart
   C. trial and error
   D. calculation

_____ 3. Power feed rates on most milling machines are expressed in terms of how far the table moves each
   A. spindle revolution
   B. minute
   C. second
   D. cutter tooth

4-7. Short Answer. Solve the following problems.

_____ 4. Calculate the correct rpm to run a ½″ [12.7 mm] diameter end mill for cutting steel at 90 fpm [27.4 mpm].

_____ 5. Calculate the correct rpm to run a 2″ [50.8 mm] shell end mill for cutting aluminum at 200 fpm [61 mpm].

_____ 6. Calculate the feed rate for a four-flute end mill of 1″ [25.4 mm] diameter, using an rpm of 360 and a feed per tooth of 0.002″ [0.05 mm].

_____ 7. Calculate the feed rate for a 3″ [76.2 mm] diameter 16-tooth plain-milling cutter, using an rpm of 120 and a feed per tooth of 0.005″ [0.127 mm].

8-10. Short Answer.

_____ 8. What is the rate at which the workpiece advances into the milling cutter called?

_____ 9. What metal rating affects cutting speed?

_____ 10. For finishing cuts, the feed should be reduced by what percentage?

UNITS 72-75
Milling Procedures

1-7. Multiple Choice. Write the letter of the correct response to each statement or question in the space at the left.

_____   1. Milling a flat surface with a milling cutter mounted on a horizontal milling machine arbor is called
A. face milling
B. surface milling
C. form milling
D. plain milling

_____   2. Milling a flat surface parallel to the face of a cutter is called
A. face milling
B. end milling
C. surface milling
D. plain milling

_____   3. An angular cut that removes only part of an edge is called a
A. bevel cut
B. slant cut
C. chamfer cut
D. angle cut

_____   4. An angular cut that completely removes a perpendicular edge is called a
A. bevel cut
B. slant cut
C. chamfer
D. angle cut

_____   5. For squaring a rectangular block, which of the following is the recommended order of machining the six surfaces?
A. face, edge, edge, face, end, end
B. face, face, edge, edge, end, end
C. face, edge, face, edge, end, end
D. edge, edge, face, face, end, end

_____   6. T-slots and dovetail slots
A. can be milled in one pass with proper cutters
B. can be made on a horizontal milling machine
C. require a plain slot to be milled first
D. cannot be made on vertical milling machines

_____   7. A boring attachment used in milling machines that can be adjusted to make different size holes is called a
A. boring bar
B. adjustable boring bar
C. boring head
D. fly cutter

(Continued on next page)

8-10. Short Answer. Solve the following problems. Write the answers in the blanks at the left.

_____

8. Calculate the distance the workpiece must be moved, dimension X in the illustration, to align its center with the center of the cutter. The cutter width is ¼" [6.35 mm], the workpiece diameter is 1" [25.4 mm], and the paper feeler is 0.003" [0.076 mm].

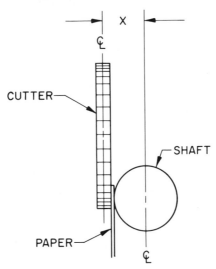

_____

9. A vertical milling machine is to be used to drill the hole in the workpiece shown. If an edge finder of 0.500" [12.7 mm] diameter is used, how far in the X axis does the milling table need to be moved in order to accurately locate the hole?

Inch	mm
.625	15.88
.875	22.23

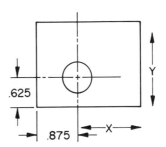

_____

10. How far in the Y axis does the milling table need to be moved in order to accurately locate the hole in question 9?

UNIT 76
Dividing or Indexing Operations

1-4. Multiple Choice. Write the letter of the correct response to each statement or question in the space to the left.

_____   1. The simplest form of indexing is called
        A. simple indexing   C. straight indexing
        B. direct indexing   D. plain indexing

_____   2. The direct index plate that is attached to the dividing head spindle has how many equally spaced holes?
        A. 12   C. 36
        B. 24   D. 40

_____   3. Most dividing heads require the index crank to be turned how many times to make the spindle revolve once?
        A. 5   C. 20
        B. 10   D. 40

_____   4. The dividing head feature that eliminates the need to count holes for partial turns of the index crank is called the
        A. fingers   C. dividers
        B. sector arms   D. bisectors

5-10. Short Answer. Calculate answers to the following indexing problems.

_____   5. Through how many spaces should the direct index plate be moved each time in order to mill a square on the end of a round rod?

_____   6. Through how many spaces should the direct index plate be moved in order to mill a hexagon on the end of a round rod?

_____   7. How many degrees does the spindle rotate when the direct index plate is moved 5 spaces?

_____   8. Simple indexing to mill a square on the end of a round rod would require the index crank to be turned how many times?

_____   9. Simple indexing to mill a 48-tooth gear would require the index crank to be turned how many times?

_____   10. Simple indexing to drill two holes 60 degrees apart would require the index crank to be turned how many times?

UNIT 77
Shaping and Planing Machines

1-6. Multiple Choice. Write the letter of the correct response to each statement or question in the space at the left.

_____   1. Shapers cut by feeding the
     A. workpiece past a tool that moves back and forth
     B. workpiece past a revolving tool
     C. tool past a workpiece that moves back and forth
     D. tool past a revolving workpiece

_____   2. Planers cut by feeding the
     A. workpiece past a tool that moves back and forth
     B. workpiece past a revolving tool
     C. tool past a workpiece that moves back and forth
     D. tool past a revolving workpiece

_____   3. Because of the work they do, vertical shapers are also known as
     A. gear shapers
     B. slotters
     C. slitters
     D. profilers

_____   4. A 14″ [356 mm] shaper is one that
     A. has a table 14″ [356 mm] square
     B. can cut a maximum length of 14″
     C. has a ram that is 14″ long
     D. can machine a 14″ cube

_____   5. The two types of planers are called
     A. double-housing and open-side
     B. horizontal and vertical
     C. plain and universal
     D. reciprocating and rotary

_____   6. Because shapers and planers are so inefficient, they have been largely replaced with
     A. lathes
     B. broaching machines
     C. milling machines
     D. all of the above

7-10. Short Answer. List four adjustments that can be made manually on a shaper without turning the machine on.

7. _____

8. _____

9. _____

10. _____

UNIT 78
Broaching Machines

1-6. Multiple Choice. Write the letter of the correct response to each statement or question in the space at the left.

_____   1. Broaching machines use specially designed cutting tools called
    A. form tools   C. punches
    B. profile tools   D. broaches

_____   2. Broaching machines usually complete the cutting operation with
    A. four strokes   C. one stroke
    B. eight strokes   D. more than ten strokes

_____   3. Broaching machines are used mostly for production machining of precision shapes
    A. on outside surfaces   C. inside holes
    B. in soft metals   D. both A and C

_____   4. Most broaches are made to cut by
    A. pulling the broach through or across   C. pushing the workpiece past the
       the workpiece   broach
    B. pushing the broach through or across   D. pulling the workpiece past the
       the workpiece   broach

_____   5. The two main types of broaching machines are
    A. plain and universal   C. external and internal
    B. reciprocating and rotary   D. horizontal and vertical

_____   6. Broaching is often done to machine complex parts because it is
    A. less costly   C. more costly
    B. less accurate   D. leaves a rough finish

7-10. Short Answer. List four types of workpieces often machined by internal broaching.

7. _____

8. _____

9. _____

10. _____

154

Name _____

Score _____

UNIT 79
Cylindrical Grinders

1-10. Multiple Choice. Write the letter of the correct response to each statement or question in the space to the left.

_____   1. When only a small amount of metal is removed by using an abrasive machine tool, it is called
    A. abrasive machining   C. precision grinding
    B. nonprecision grinding   D. grinding

_____   2. Removing large amounts of metal with abrasive machine tools is called
    A. abrasive machining   C. nonprecision grinding
    B. grinding   D. precision grinding

_____   3. Many kinds of precision metal parts require grinding to tolerances as fine as plus or minus
    A. 0.100″ [2.54 mm]   C. 0.001″ [0.025 mm]
    B. 0.010″ [0.254 mm]   D. 0.0001″ [0.0025 mm]

_____   4. Rough cuts on a cylindrical grinder are about how deep?
    A. 0.0002″ [0.005 mm] to 0.001″ [0.025 mm]   C. 0.004″ [0.10 mm] to 0.008″ [0.2 mm]
                                                D. 0.008″ [0.2 mm] to 0.012″ [0.3 mm]
    B. 0.001″ [0.025 mm] to 0.004″ [0.10 mm]

_____   5. Finish cuts on cylindrical grinding machines are about how deep?
    A. 0.0002″ [0.005 mm] to 0.001″ [0.025 mm]   C. 0.004″ [0.10 mm] to 0.008″ [0.2 mm]
                                                D. 0.008″ [0.2 mm] to 0.012″ [0.3 mm]
    B. 0.001″ [0.025 mm] to 0.004″ [0.10 mm]

_____   6. Plain cylindrical grinding machines can grind
    A. cylindrical surfaces   C. cylindrical surfaces, shallow tapers, and steep tapers
    B. cylindrical surfaces and shallow tapers   D. cylindrical surfaces, shallow and steep tapers, internal cylinders and cones

_____   7. Universal cylindrical grinding machines can grind
    A. straight shafts   C. straight shafts, shallow tapers, and steep tapers
    B. straight shafts and shallow tapers   D. straight shafts, shallow and steep tapers, internal cylinders and cones

(Continued on next page)

_____ 8. A type of cylindrical grinding machine that has no provision for holding the workpiece in a chuck or between centers is the
A. plain cylindrical grinder
B. universal cylindrical grinder
C. centerless grinder
D. tool and cutter grinder

_____ 9. Grinding with a wheel cut so that it will grind a special shape on a workpiece is called
A. contour grinding
B. profile grinding
C. shape grinding
D. form grinding

_____ 10. For form grinding, the wheel is cut to shape with a(n)
A. internal grinding attachment
B. diamond dressing tool
C. cutter
D. none of the above

UNIT 80
Tool and Cutter Grinders

1-5. Multiple Choice. Write the letter of the correct response to each statement or question in the space at the left.

_____ 1. The type of grinding machine made for sharpening precision tools such as milling cutters, reamers, etc., is the
A. plain cylindrical grinder   C. tool and cutter grinder
B. universal cylindrical grinder   D. pedestal grinder

_____ 2. Which grinding wheel shape(s) is (are) used for sharpening milling cutters?
A. flaring cup   C. convex-concave
B. plain disc   D. A and B

_____ 3. Form-relieved milling cutters such as gear and radius cutters are
A. sharpened by grinding the tooth face   C. thrown away when dull
B. sharpened by grinding the curved   D. both A and B
   profile

_____ 4. In order to obtain the necessary clearance when sharpening milling cutters with disc wheels,
A. the tooth rest is set to the same   C. the tooth rest is set to the same
   height as the cutter center, and the   height as the grinding wheel center,
   grinding wheel center is offset   and the cutter is offset
B. the grinding wheel is set to the same D. A or B
   height as the cutter, and the tooth
   rest is offset

_____ 5. In order to obtain the necessary clearance when sharpening milling cutters with cup wheels,
A. the tooth rest is set to the same   C. the tooth rest is set to the same
   height as the cutter center, and the   height as the grinding wheel center,
   grinding wheel is offset   and the cutter is offset
B. the grinding wheel is set to the same D. A or C
   height as the cutter, and the tooth
   rest is offset

6-7. Short Answer. Name two tools that can be sharpened on a tool and cutter grinding machine.

6. _____

7. _____

(Continued on next page)

8-10. Short Answer. List three things that might happen when a cutting tool becomes dull.

8. _____

9. _____

10. _____

UNIT 81
Surface-Grinding Machines

1-4. Matching. Match each of the types of surface grinders pictured with their names by writing the correct letters in the blanks.

_____   1. Horizontal spindle, reciprocating table

_____   2. Horizontal spindle, rotary table

_____   3. Vertical spindle, reciprocating table

_____   4. Vertical spindle, rotary table

A

B

C

D

(Continued on next page)

5-10. Multiple Choice. Write the letter of the correct response to each statement or question in the space to the left.

_____ 5. A 6″ × 18″ [152 × 457 mm] surface grinder is one that
A. has a grinding wheel that size
B. has a vertical and cross feed that size
C. has a vertical and longitudinal feed that size
D. can grind a flat surface that size

_____ 6. Flat iron and steel parts of medium size are usually held for surface grinding
A. by clamping them to the grinder table
B. in a vise
C. on a magnetic chuck
D. in V-blocks

_____ 7. Flat iron and steel parts of small size are most safely held for surface grinding
A. on a magnetic chuck
B. in a vise
C. by clamping to the grinder table
D. all of the above

_____ 8. Angled surfaces can be surface-ground by holding the workpiece in a
A. plain vise
B. swivel vise
C. tilting vise
D. all of the above

_____ 9. Which type of grinder table moves back and forth?
A. rotary
B. reciprocating
C. horizontal
D. shifting

_____ 10. The size of a surface grinding machine is determined by the size of the
A. grinding wheel
B. chuck
C. working area of the table
D. base

Name _____

Score _____

UNIT 82
Surface Grinding with Horizontal-Spindle Surface-Grinding Machines

1-7. Multiple Choice. Write the letter of the correct response to each statement or question in the space to the left.

_____   1. For average rough cuts on small surface grinders, the recommended cross feed for each cut is
A. 0.030″ to 0.050″ [0.76 to 1.27 mm]   C. 0.100″ to 0.200″ [2.54 to 5.08 mm]
B. 0.050″ to 0.100″ [1.27 to 2.54 mm]   D. 0.200″ to 0.500″ [5.08 to 12.7 mm]

_____   2. For finishing cuts on small surface grinders, the recommended cross feed for each cut is
A. 0.030″ to 0.050″ [0.76 to 1.27 mm]   C. 0.100″ to 0.200″ [2.54 to 5.08 mm]
B. 0.050″ to 0.100″ [1.27 to 2.54 mm]   D. 0.200″ to 0.500″ [5.08 to 12.7 mm]

_____   3. Roughing cuts on a surface grinder should be how deep?
A. 0.200″ to 0.300″ [5.08 to 7.62 mm]   C. 0.002″ to 0.003″ [0.05 to 0.08 mm]
B. 0.020″ to 0.030″ [0.51 to 0.76 mm]   D. 0.0002″ to 0.0003″ [0.005 to 0.008 mm]

_____   4. Finishing cuts on a surface grinder are usually how deep?
A. 0.0001″ [0.0025 mm] or less   C. 0.010″ [0.25 mm] or less
B. 0.001″ [0.025 mm] or less   D. 0.100″ [2.54 mm] or less

_____   5. When using a coolant during surface grinding, the coolant should be turned on
A. before the grinding wheel and turned off after the grinding wheel   C. after the grinding wheel and turned off after the grinding wheel
B. after the grinding wheel and turned off before the grinding wheel   D. before the grinding wheel and turned off before the grinding wheel

_____   6. Dressing a grinding wheel means to
A. recoat the wheel with new abrasive grains   C. restore concentricity
B. reshape the wheel   D. resharpen the wheel

_____   7. Truing a grinding wheel means to
A. resharpen it   C. reshape it
B. restore concentricity   D. both B and C

(Continued on next page)

8-10. Short Answer.

_____ 8. What is used to raise or lower the grinding wheel?

_____ 9. What is used to set the length of table travel?

_____ 10. What is the term for cutting the wheel so no high spots occur when the wheel is running?

Name _____

Score _____

UNIT 83
Electrical Discharge Machining (EDM)

1-9. Multiple Choice. Write the letter of the correct response to each statement or question in the space to the left.

_____   1. The machining process that removes metal by controlled electrical arcing under an insulating fluid is called
     A. spark forming   C. electrical discharge machining
     B. electroforming   D. electrical arc machining

_____   2. Electrical discharge machining **is not** capable of which one of the following?
     A. cutting metals of any hardness   C. machining complex shapes
     B. machining delicate workpieces   D. cutting materials that **do not** conduct electricity

_____   3. Electrical discharge machining is widely used in
     A. high volume production   C. repair work
     B. research and development   D. mold and die making

_____   4. The type of electrical discharge machine that has revolutionized the cutting of blanking dies for sheet metal stamping is the type that uses
     A. stationary wire electrodes   C. solid rotating electrodes
     B. a traveling wire electrode   D. solid nonrotating electrodes

_____   5. One of the materials commonly used for solid electrical discharge machining electrodes is
     A. aluminum   C. graphite
     B. lead   D. nickel

_____   6. The most commonly used electrical discharge machining dielectric fluid is
     A. alcohol   C. deionized water
     B. thin petroleum oil   D. thin silicone oil

_____   7. The electric arc is created between the tool and the
     A. table   C. electrode
     B. traveling wire   D. workpiece

_____   8. Traveling wire electrode machines have revolutionized the cutting of
     A. blanking dies   C. honeycomb structures
     B. plastics   D. stepped tools

_____   9. The purpose of dielectric fluid is to
     A. reduce electric shock   C. cool the machine
     B. increase feed rate   D. wash away chips

Name _____

Score _____

UNIT 84
Electrochemical Machining (ECM)

1-8. Multiple Choice. Write the letter of the correct response to each statement or question in the space to the left.

_____   1. A machining process that is the reverse of electroplating is
   A. chemical milling   C. electrochemical machining
   B. electroforming   D. electrical discharge machining

_____   2. Electrodes for electrochemical machining are commonly made of
   A. copper and brass   C. cast iron
   B. low-carbon steel   D. silver

_____   3. Which one of the following **is not** an advantage of electrochemical machining?
   A. high metal removal rates   C. bright and smooth finishes
   B. burr-free machining   D. no tool pressure on the workpiece

_____   4. Electrochemical machining is limited to cutting materials that
   A. are hard   C. do not conduct electricity
   B. are soft   D. conduct electricity

_____   5. Electrochemical machining is also used for
   A. electrochemical sawing   C. electrochemical grinding
   B. electrochemical deburring   D. both B and C

_____   6. Compared to conventional machining methods, ECM rates are
   A. slower   B. faster

_____   7. In ECM the workpiece becomes the
   A. cathode   B. anode

_____   8. During ECM, the current causes metal particles to be dissolved into the
   A. dielectric fluid   C. electrolyte
   B. cutting fluid   D. surrounding air

9-10. Short Answer. Because there is no tool pressure, what types of workpieces are best machined by ECM?

9. _____

10. _____

Name _____

Score _____

UNIT 85
Electron Beam Machining (EBM)

1-6. Multiple Choice. Write the letter of the correct response to each statement or question in the space to the left.

_____ 1. The cutting tool used in electron beam machining is a(n)
   A. intense beam of light
   B. high-speed arc of electricity
   C. high-speed beam of electrons
   D. high-speed stream of abrasive

_____ 2. Electron beam machining can cut
   A. only materials that conduct electricity
   B. only materials with low melting points
   C. any known material
   D. only materials that do not conduct electricity

_____ 3. Electron beam machining is used mostly for
   A. cutting thick, soft materials
   B. cutting thick, hard materials
   C. rapid blanking of small sheet metal parts
   D. cutting tiny holes or slots in thin, hard-to-machine materials

_____ 4. Electron beam machining **is not** widely used because
   A. equipment cost is very high
   B. highly trained operators are needed
   C. X-ray shielding is required
   D. all of the above

_____ 5. During EBM, the metal on the workpiece is
   A. vaporized
   B. dissolved in electrolyte
   C. removed by freezing
   D. chemically dissolved

_____ 6. The beam is directed into patterns by means of a(n)
   A. electrode wire
   B. vacuum
   C. magnetic deflection coil
   D. lens

7-10. Short Answer. List the four disadvantages of EBM.

7. _____

8. _____

9. _____

10. _____

Name _____

Score _____

UNIT 86
Laser Beam Machining (LBM)

1-7. Multiple Choice. Write the letter of the correct response to each statement or question in the space to the left.

_____   1. A machining method that uses a concentrated beam of light as the cutting tool is called
               A. light beam machining   C. maser beam machining
               B. laser beam machining   D. electron beam machining

_____   2. Lasers that can produce a continuous laser beam are of which type?
               A. solid   C. gas
               B. liquid   D. A and C

_____   3. The cutting capacity of laser cutting systems is increased by using
               A. carbon dioxide   C. nitrogen
               B. oxygen   D. hydrogen

_____   4. Lasers are used to do
               A. scribing and engraving   C. heat-treating and welding
               B. hole-drilling and cutting   D. all of the above

_____   5. Laser beams can cut
               A. only materials that conduct electricity   C. only materials with low melting points
               B. only materials that do not conduct electricity   D. any known material

_____   6. Laser systems that use oxygen can cut mild steel up to what thickness?
               A. ½ inch   C. 1 inch
               B. ⅜ inch   D. 2 inches

_____   7. Lasers capable of only short bursts of power are which type?
               A. gas   B. solid

8-10. Short Answer. For what jobs is the gas laser best suited?

8. _____

9. _____

10. _____

UNIT 87
Ultrasonic Machining (USM)

1-7. Multiple Choice. Write the letter of the correct response to each statement or question in the space to the left.

_____   1. Ultrasonic machining removes material
      A. with sound waves   C. by friction between tool and work-
      B. by bombarding the workpiece with   piece
         abrasive grains   D. with compressed air

_____   2. A special advantage of ultrasonic machining is that
      A. tool wear is low   C. it can cut materials that do not con-
      B. cutting rates are high   duct electricity
                                        D. it can cut materials of any hardness

_____   3. Tools for ultrasonic machining are usually made of
      A. soft steel   C. high-speed steel
      B. brass   D. A or B

_____   4. Ultrasonic machining is also known as
      A. abrasive machining   C. vibratory machining
      B. sand blasting   D. impact grinding

_____   5. The abrasive used in ultrasonic machining is
      A. aluminum oxide   C. boron carbide
      B. silicon carbide   D. all of the above

_____   6. In which fluid are the abrasive particles suspended?
      A. oil   C. electrolyte
      B. water   D. brine

_____   7. Grit sizes range from _____ mesh.
      A. 280-800   C. 75-150
      B. 700-900   D. 400-600

8-10. Short Answer. Name three materials machined by USM that cannot be machined by EDM, ECM, or ECG.

8. _____

9. _____

10. _____

Name _____

Score _____

UNIT 88
Chemical Machining (CHM)

1-10. Multiple Choice. Write the letter of the correct response to each statement or question in the space to the left.

_____   1. In chemical milling, metal is removed by
  A. acid solutions   C. abrasive solutions
  B. alkaline solutions   D. A or B

_____   2. Using acids to cut shapes from thin sheet metal is called chemical
  A. shaping   C. milling
  B. cutting   D. blanking

_____   3. Chemical milling is most widely used in what industry?
  A. appliance   C. electrical/electronic
  B. automotive   D. aerospace

_____   4. Which one of the following **is not** an advantage of chemical milling?
  A. rapid metal removal from complex   C. no operator hazards
     shapes   D. capability to machine thin, delicate
  B. skilled labor not needed   workpieces

_____   5. The acid-resistant coating that protects areas of parts from being attacked by the chemical milling solution is made of
  A. neoprene rubber   C. vinyl plastic
  B. masking tape   D. A or C

_____   6. The first step in chemical blanking is to make a _____ of the part.
  A. photoresist   C. mold
  B. drawing   D. copy

_____   7. The acid-resistant coating for chemical blanking is called a
  A. photoresist   C. screen
  B. mask   D. any of the above

_____   8. For chemical milling, the acid-resistant coating is cured by
  A. soaking in brine   C. baking
  B. soaking in water   D. freezing

_____   9. Chemical milling is used mainly in the _____ industries.
  A. automobile   C. electronic
  B. graphic arts   D. aerospace

_____ 10. Chemical blanking is used to make
  A. printed circuit boards   C. aerospace machinery
  B. photographic equipment   D. auto parts

UNIT 89
Miscellaneous Machining Processes

1-10. Multiple Choice. Write the letter of the correct response to each statement or question in the space to the left.

_____ 1. The abrasive machining process that is used for resistor trimming, scribing of hard metals, deburring, and etching of glass and ceramics is
A. abrasive flow machining
B. ultrasonic machining
C. abrasive jet machining
D. sand blasting

_____ 2. An abrasive machining process that is used mainly for deburring and polishing hard-to-reach edges and surfaces inside workpieces is
A. ultrasonic machining
B. abrasive flow machining
C. abrasive jet machining
D. electrochemical machining

_____ 3. The abrasives generally used in abrasive jet and abrasive flow machining are
A. emery and silicon carbide
B. aluminum oxide and boron carbide
C. boron carbide and diamond
D. aluminum oxide and silicon carbide

_____ 4. A plasma arc torch can produce temperatures as high as
A. 5,000° F [2,760° C]
B. 10,000° F [5,538° C]
C. 20,000° F [11,100° C]
D. 50,000° F [27,760° C]

_____ 5. Plasma arc machining is used mostly for
A. cutting thin carbon-steel sheet
B. cutting thick carbon-steel sheet
C. cutting metals that cannot be cut with oxyacetylene torches
D. making holes in very hard metals

_____ 6. Pressures used in water jet cutting reach
A. 20,000 psi (137.9 MPa)
B. 40,000 psi (275.79 MPa)
C. 60,000 psi (413.69 MPa)
D. 80,000 psi (551.58 MPa)

_____ 7. For water jet cutting of most metals
A. filtered water is used
B. ionized water is used
C. abrasives are added to the stream of water before it leaves the nozzle
D. abrasives are added to the stream of water after it leaves the nozzle

_____ 8. On some materials, water jet cutting speeds may be as high as
A. 250 inches/minute (6.35 m/minute)
B. 500 inches/minute (12.7 m/minute)
C. 1000 inches/minute (25.4 m/minute)
D. 1500 inches/minute (38.1 m/minute)

(Continued on next page)

_____ 9. Water jet cutting can cut titanium up to _____ inch(es) thick.
    A. one   C. three
    B. two   D. four

_____ 10. The PAM process is used mainly for cutting metals that cannot be cut with oxy-acetylene torches or
    A. water jet cutting   C. lasers
    B. electron beams   D. plasma arc

UNIT 90
Principles of Automation

1-8. Matching. Match the terms and definitions by writing the correct letters in the blanks.

_____ 1. Automatic

_____ 2. Automation

_____ 3. Input

_____ 4. Output

_____ 5. Sensor

_____ 6. Control center

_____ 7. Open-loop feedback system

_____ 8. Closed-loop feedback system

A. A device that detects and reports some aspect of a machine or process output.
B. A feedback system that automatically adjusts output to match input instructions.
C. Self-acting.
D. The work produced by a machine operation or process.
E. Commands, data, or standards specifying the output.
F. A feedback system that cannot automatically adjust output to match input instructions.
G. A device that compares output information with input commands, then issues instructions to control the process.
H. Automatic operation and adjustment of machines, equipment, or processes without human aid.

9-10. Short Answer. As metalworking becomes more and more automated, for what jobs will people be needed? (Name two.)

9. _____

10. _____

UNIT 91

Introduction to Numerical Control (N/C)

1-8. Multiple Choice. Write the letter of the correct response to each statement or question in the space to the left.

_____   1. Instructions to numerically controlled machines are provided by
   A. punched tape
   B. a large computer that can control several machines at the same time
   C. a microcomputer at the machine
   D. any of the above

_____   2. Which one of the following **is not** an advantage of using N/C machines?
   A. N/C is ideal for high-volume, long-run production of simple cylindrical parts.
   B. Only simple workholding fixtures are needed.
   C. Fewer parts are spoiled because of human error.
   D. Design changes can be made quickly by changing the N/C program.

_____   3. Which axis of the Cartesian coordinate system is always assigned to the machine spindle?
   A. Z
   B. Y
   C. X
   D. W

_____   4. Point-to-point N/C systems usually are programmed only for straight-line moves parallel to an axis and
   A. any angle
   B. 45-degree angles
   C. curves with a constant radius
   D. irregular curves

_____   5. Contouring N/C systems can be programmed for straight-line moves parallel to an axis and
   A. any angle
   B. curves with a constant radius
   C. irregular curves
   D. all of the above

_____   6. Preparation of the N/C manuscript and tape is usually the responsibility of the
   A. N/C machine operator
   B. design engineer
   C. N/C programmer
   D. layout worker

_____   7. A dry run of an N/C program is a trial run
   A. with a workpiece in position
   B. without a workpiece in position

_____   8. A test run of an N/C program is a trial run that is done
   A. with a workpiece in position
   B. using all the cutting tools required
   C. after a dry run has been made
   D. all of the above

9. Short Answer. What is the name for the system of rectangular coordinates used as the basis for N/C measurements?

9. _____

UNIT 92
Numerical Control Programming

1-6. Multiple Choice. Write the letter of the correct response to each statement or question in the space to the left.

_____ 1. The kind of dimensioning system in which all measurements are made from a common reference point is called
A. unidimensional
B. absolute
C. incremental
D. independent

_____ 2. The kind of dimensioning system in which measurements are made between points **without** reference to a fixed point is called
A. unidimensional
B. absolute
C. incremental
D. independent

_____ 3. The kind of N/C programming format that uses a letter followed by the numerical data is called
A. letter address
B. tab sequential
C. word address
D. code address

_____ 4. The N/C programming system that can remember feed rates of machining cycles from one block to another until they are cancelled is the
A. variable-block
B. full-block
C. fixed-sequence
D. variable-sequence

_____ 5. When preparing to write an N/C program, which one of the following should be decided first?
A. where to place the setup point
B. where to locate the workpiece on the machine table
C. how the workpiece will be held for machining
D. the order in which the machining operations will be done

_____ 6. For an N/C system that uses the minus sign for negative direction moves, the program should be written as though the
A. tool were moving over the workpiece
B. workpiece were moving past the tool

(Continued on next page)

7-10. Short Answer. Write the N/C programs necessary to machine the following parts. Use incremental variable block programming in word address form.

7. _____

_____

_____

_____

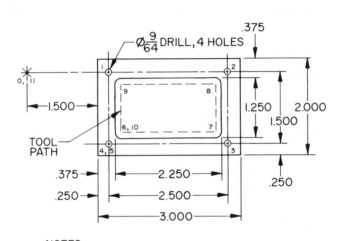

Inch	mm
9/64	3.57
.250	6.35
.375	9.53
1.250	31.75
1.500	38.10
2.000	50.80
2.250	57.15
3.000	76.20

8. _____

_____

_____

_____

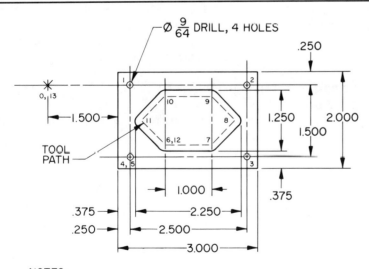

Inch	mm
9/64	3.57
.250	6.35
.375	9.53
1.000	25.40
1.250	31.75
1.500	38.10
2.000	50.80
2.250	57.15
2.500	63.50
3.000	76.20

9. _____

_____

_____

_____

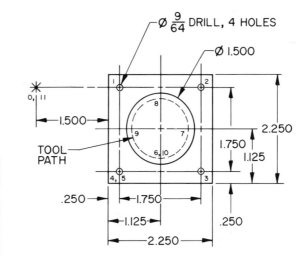

Inch	mm
9/64	3.57
.250	6.35
1.125	28.58
1.500	38.10
1.750	44.45
2.250	57.15

NOTES:
1. STEP 5 IS A TOOL CHANGE.
2. MILL OPENING WITH A 1/4" END MILL.

10. _____

_____

_____

_____

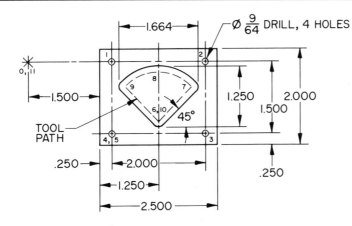

Inch	mm
9/64	3.57
.250	6.35
1.250	31.75
1.500	38.10
1.664	42.27
2.000	50.80
2.500	63.50

NOTES:
1. STEP 5 IS A TOOL CHANGE.
2. MILL OPENING WITH A 1/4" END MILL.

(Continued on next page)

11-14. Short Answer. Write the N/C programs necessary to machine the pictured parts (finish cut only). Use absolute variable block programming in word address form. Assume a zero tool nose radius. The zero point is the centerline of the machine in the X-axis and the end of the workpiece in the Z-axis.

11. _____

_____

_____

_____

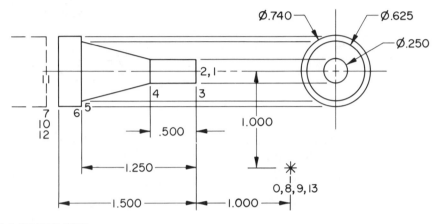

Inch	mm
.250	6.35
.500	12.70
.625	15.88
.740	18.80
.750	19.05
1.000	25.40
1.250	31.75
1.500	38.10

NOTES:
1. PROGRAM IN ABSOLUTE
2. STEP 9 IS A TOOL CHANGE TO A CUTOFF TOOL.
3. NUMBERED PROGRAM SEQUENCE IS FOR FINISH CUT AND CUTOFF ONLY. CONSULT WITH YOUR INSTRUCTOR AS TO WHETHER ROUGH CUTS SHOULD BE PROGRAMMED.

12. _____

_____

_____

_____

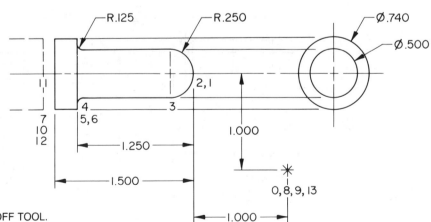

Inch	mm
.125	3.18
.250	6.35
.500	12.70
.740	18.80
1.000	25.40
1.250	31.75
1.500	38.10

NOTES:
1. PROGRAM IN ABSOLUTE.
2. STEP 9 IS A TOOL CHANGE TO A CUTOFF TOOL.
3. NUMBERED PROGRAM SEQUENCE IS FOR FINISH CUT AND CUTOFF ONLY. CONSULT WITH YOUR INSTRUCTOR AS TO WHETHER ROUGH CUTS SHOULD BE PROGRAMMED.

13. _____

_____

_____

_____

_____

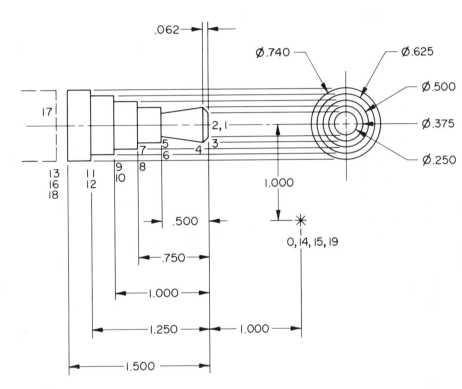

Inch	mm
.062	1.57
.250	6.35
.375	9.53
.500	12.70
.625	15.88
.740	18.80
.750	19.05
1.000	25.40
1.250	31.75
1.500	38.10

NOTES:
1. PROGRAM IN ABSOLUTE.
2. STEP 15 IS A TOOL CHANGE TO A CUTOFF TOOL.
3. NUMBERED PROGRAM SEQUENCE IS FOR FINISH CUT AND CUTOFF ONLY. CONSULT WITH YOUR INSTRUCTOR AS TO WHETHER ROUGH CUTS SHOULD BE PROGRAMMED.

177

14. _____
_____
_____
_____
_____
_____
_____
_____
_____

Inch	mm
.062	1.57
.150	3.81
.625	15.88
.740	18.80
1.000	25.40
1.250	31.75
1.500	38.10
3.500	88.90

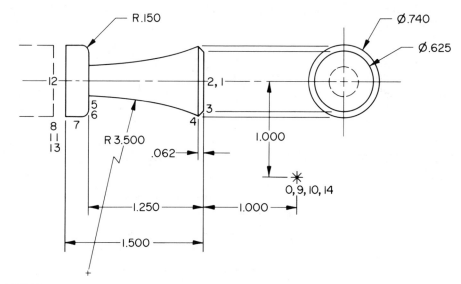

NOTES:
1. PROGRAM IN ABSOLUTE.
2. STEP 10 IS A TOOL CHANGE TO A CUTOFF TOOL.
3. NUMBERED PROGRAM SEQUENCE IS FOR FINISH CUT AND CUTOFF ONLY. CONSULT WITH YOUR INSTRUCTOR AS TO WHETHER ROUGH CUTS SHOULD BE PROGRAMMED.

UNIT 93
Inspection Tools and Equipment

1-9. Multiple Choice. Write the letter of the correct response to each statement or question in the space to the left.

_____ 1. A successful program of quality control requires
A. accurate inspection
B. statistical process control
C. scientific sampling methods
D. all of the above

_____ 2. Official examination of materials, parts, and finished products is called
A. assessment
B. checking
C. inspection
D. quality control

_____ 3. Making parts with such accuracy that they can be replaced with other parts taken from another product of the same make and model is called
A. replaceability
B. interchangeability
C. precision manufacturing
D. parts duplication

_____ 4. What is the practical standard for measurement used in industrial plants all around the world?
A. the international Prototype Meter
B. micrometers
C. gage blocks
D. vernier calipers

_____ 5. Class 1 gage blocks have an accuracy of
A. ±0.000 001″ [0.025 microns]
B. ±0.000 002″ [0.05 microns]
C. +0.000 004″ [0.10 microns]
   −0.000 002″ [0.05 microns]
D. +0.000 008″ [0.20 microns]
   −0.000 004″ [0.10 microns]

_____ 6. Gages designed for measuring a certain range of dimensions are called
A. fixed gages
B. limits gages
C. variable gages
D. adjustable gages

_____ 7. Gages that are used to check the accuracy of other gages are called
A. reference gages
B. inspection gages
C. master gages
D. either A or C

_____ 8. The inspection device that projects an enlarged shadow-like profile of the object being measured onto a screen where it is compared to a master drawing is the
A. optical flat
B. optical magnifier
C. optical comparator
D. microscope

_____ 9. The inspection device that is used to measure extremely flat surfaces is the
A. optical flat
B. surface plate
C. optical comparator
D. microscope

(Continued on next page)

10-21. Matching. Match the gages pictured with their names by writing the correct letters in the blanks.

_____ 10. Plain plug gage

_____ 11. Thread ring gage

_____ 12. Snap gage

_____ 13. Taper plug gage

_____ 14. Radius gage

_____ 15. Screw pitch gage

_____ 16. Thickness gage

_____ 17. Dial comparator

_____ 18. Universal dial indicator

_____ 19. Air gage

_____ 20. Electronic gage

_____ 21. Optical flat

A

B

C

D

E

F

G

H

I

J

K

L

Name _Justin Stilwell_

Score _____

UNIT 94
Destructive and Nondestructive Testing

1-13. Multiple Choice. Write the letter of the correct response to each statement or question in the space to the left.

_C_   1. A test that determines the force required to pull a standard sample of metal apart is known as a(n)
    A. torsion test   C. tensile test
    B. impact test   D. compression test

_B_   2. A test that determines the force required to break a standard sample of metal apart with a hammer blow is known as a(n)
    A. torsion test   C. compression test
    B. impact test   D. tensile test

_C_   3. A test that determines the number of bending cycles a standard sample of metal can withstand before it cracks is known as a
    A. bend test   C. fatigue test
    B. guided bend test   D. ductility test

_D_   4. Bend tests, guided bend tests, and cup-drawing tests are done to determine what metal property?
    A. fatigue limit   C. impact strength
    B. tensile strength   D. ductility

_B_   5. The testing of metal to determine its resistance to attack by liquids or atmospheres is called
    A. abrasion testing   C. wear testing
    B. corrosion testing   D. property testing

_C_   6. The Rockwell hardness scale that is used to test hardened steels is the
    A. A scale   C. C scale
    B. B scale   D. N scale

_C_   7. The kind of hardness tester that requires a microscope to measure the diameter of the indentation, which is then converted into a hardness number, is the
    A. Rockwell   C. Brinell
    B. Shore Scleroscope   D. Vickers

_B_   8. The kind of hardness tester that measures the rebound of a diamond-tipped hammer is the
    A. Rockwell   C. Brinell
    B. Shore Scleroscope   D. Knoop

(Continued on next page)

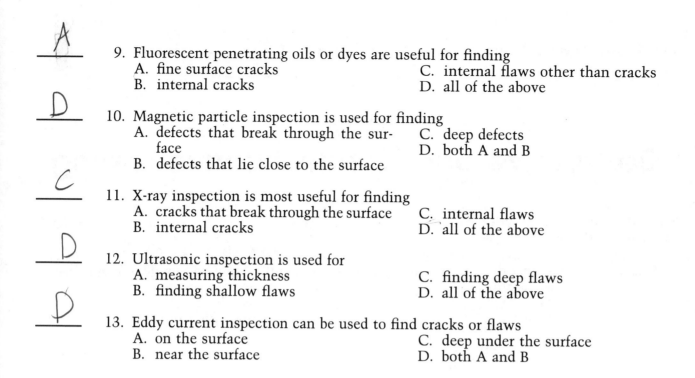

_A_ 9. Fluorescent penetrating oils or dyes are useful for finding
    A. fine surface cracks   C. internal flaws other than cracks
    B. internal cracks   D. all of the above

_D_ 10. Magnetic particle inspection is used for finding
    A. defects that break through the sur-   C. deep defects
       face   D. both A and B
    B. defects that lie close to the surface

_C_ 11. X-ray inspection is most useful for finding
    A. cracks that break through the surface   C. internal flaws
    B. internal cracks   D. all of the above

_D_ 12. Ultrasonic inspection is used for
    A. measuring thickness   C. finding deep flaws
    B. finding shallow flaws   D. all of the above

_D_ 13. Eddy current inspection can be used to find cracks or flaws
    A. on the surface   C. deep under the surface
    B. near the surface   D. both A and B

Name _____

Score _____

UNIT 95
Development of Manufacturing Technology

1-20. Multiple Choice. Write the letter of the correct response to each statement or question in the space at the left.

_____ 1. It is generally agreed that the industrial revolution began with the invention of
A. the spring-driven clock in 1550
B. the steam engine in 1776
C. interchangeable parts manufacturing in 1798
D. inexpensive Bessemer steel in 1856

_____ 2. The first person to propose making interchangeable parts for guns was
A. Chauncy Jerome
B. Simeon North
C. Eli Whitney
D. Eli Terry

_____ 3. The first known true milling machine was introduced by
A. Eli Whitney
B. Simeon North
C. Eli Terry
D. Chauncy Jerome

_____ 4. The first clockmaker to adopt Simeon North's methods of manufacture was
A. Edward Barlow
B. Chauncy Jerome
C. William Clement
D. Eli Terry

_____ 5. The universal grinding machine was invented by
A. Joseph Brown in 1880
B. Brown and Sharpe in 1880
C. Andrew Shanks in 1860
D. Henry Maudslay in 1797

_____ 6. The first multiple spindle automatic lathe was invented by
A. Henry Maudslay in 1797
B. Christopher Spencer in 1873
C. Joseph Brown in 1876
D. Steven Fitch in 1845

_____ 7. All of the basic machine tools had been invented by
A. the end of the 19th century
B. the end of the Middle Ages
C. 1800
D. 1750

_____ 8. The original inventor of the micrometer was
A. James Watt
B. Brown and Sharpe
C. Carl Johansson
D. James Palmer

_____ 9. Gage blocks, the practical standard of precision measurement still used today, were invented by
A. Eli Whitney
B. David Brown
C. Carl Johansson
D. Henry Ford

(Continued on next page)

10. Automatic machines are considered to be the direct outgrowth of the development of
    A. the steam engine
    B. clocks
    C. the water wheel
    D. the American system of manufacturing

11. An automatic machine for making straight pins used in sewing was invented by John Howe in
    A. 1822
    B. 1832
    C. 1842
    D. 1852

12. Special machines that can perform all the machining operations on a part by automatically moving it between workstations are called
    A. automatons
    B. conveying machines
    C. automatics
    D. transfer machines

13. The term "automation" was first used by Delmar Harder, a vice president of Ford Motor Company, in
    A. 1937
    B. 1947
    C. 1957
    D. 1967

14. Automated machines that can manufacture only one product are referred to as
    A. limited automation
    B. soft automation
    C. hard automation
    D. simple automation

15. The first flexible manufacturing system consisted of machines for
    A. broaching and tapping
    B. grinding and drilling
    C. milling, drilling, tapping, and boring
    D. boring and grinding

16. Flexible manufacturing systems are designed around what kind of machine tools?
    A. manually operated
    B. automatic
    C. transfer
    D. computer numerically controlled

17. Electronic probes used on CNC machines can
    A. identify the workpiece and its location
    B. select the correct N/C program to machine the part
    C. inspect the part after machining and automatically correct the N/C program if necessary
    D. all of the above

18. Because many different parts can be made on flexible manufacturing systems, they are known as a type of
    A. soft automation
    B. hard automation
    C. transfer machine
    D. universal automation

19. The use of moving assembly lines for complex products was pioneered by
    A. Eli Whitney
    B. Simeon North
    C. Eli Terry
    D. Henry Ford

20. Using computers to control all aspects of a manufacturing operation is referred to as
    A. computer aided design (CAD)
    B. computer aided design and manufacturing (CADM)
    C. computer aided manufacturing (CAM)
    D. computer integrated manufacturing (CIM)

Name _____

Score _____

UNIT 96
Industrial Organization

1-4. Multiple Choice. Write the letter of the correct response to each statement or question in the space at the left.

_____ 1. The form of organization used by all large companies is the
A. staff organization C. line and staff organization
B. line organization D. none of the above

_____ 2. The line of authority in a company is shown through the use of a(n)
A. organization manual C. organization chart
B. standard practice manual D. standard practice chart

_____ 3. The company organization document that provides a detailed outline of the duties and responsibilities of each company officer is the
A. organization manual C. organization chart
B. standard practice manual D. standard practice chart

_____ 4. Company policy and standard procedure for carrying out all aspects of company operations are provided in a document known as a(n)
A. organization manual C. standard practice manual
B. organization chart D. standard practice chart

5-11. Short Answer. List the seven areas of activity in which a company must have knowledge and make skillful decisions in order to be successful.

5. _____

6. _____

7. _____

8. _____

9. _____

10. _____

11. _____

UNIT 97
Product Engineering

1-8. Multiple Choice. Write the letter of the correct response to each statement or question in the space at the left.

_____ 1. The type of engineers responsible for selecting the most suitable materials and manufacturing processes for producing a product are
  A. mechanical engineers   C. chemical engineers
  B. electrical engineers   D. civil engineers

_____ 2. The mechanical design of product components is normally done by a
  A. product designer   C. manufacturing engineer
  B. mechanical engineer   D. draftsperson

_____ 3. Hundreds of hours of actual testing of product components can now be saved by using _____ software.
  A. CADD   C. CAE
  B. CAM   D. CIM

_____ 4. The final design of consumer products is usually done by a _____ skilled in art.
  A. product designer   C. mechanical engineer
  B. draftsperson   D. manufacturing engineer

_____ 5. A full-size working model of a new product that is made to determine its suitability for manufacture is called a
  A. scale model   C. test model
  B. pre-production model   D. prototype

_____ 6. Which software system does a mechanical engineer use to create a mechanical design?
  A. CADD   C. CIM
  B. CAE   D. CAM

_____ 7. A prototype helps engineers
  A. learn possible difficulties in constructing the product   C. by providing a model for performance testing
  B. study the design   D. all of the above

_____ 8. After the prototype has been tested, the _____ is/are made.
  A. model   C. design
  B. working drawings   D. all of the above

9-10. Short Answer. On the basis of what two factors do mechanical engineers select materials?

9. _____

10. _____

Name _____

Score _____

UNIT 98
Manufacturing Process Design

1-8. Multiple Choice. Write the letter of the correct response to each statement or question in the space at the left.

_____ 1. The main purpose of manufacturing process design is to
    A. determine the quality of the product
    B. determine the quantity of the product
    C. determine the most economical method of producing the product
    D. create new methods of processing materials

_____ 2. In general, as product volume increases, the production cost per unit
    A. remains about the same
    B. increases
    C. decreases
    D. none of the above

_____ 3. In general, as the quality of a product increases, the cost per unit
    A. remains about the same
    B. increases
    C. decreases
    D. increases at first, then decreases

_____ 4. Products that can be produced much faster than they can be sold are produced in batches known as a(n)
    A. economical manufacturing lot size
    B. standard production quantity
    C. basic batch quantity
    D. cost-effective lot size

_____ 5. The kind of manufacturing used for high-volume production of such items as automobiles and appliances is
    A. continuous
    B. intermittent
    C. job-lot
    D. custom

_____ 6. The most important of the process design communication and record forms is the
    A. standard process sheet
    B. flow process sheet
    C. job ticket
    D. working drawing

_____ 7. The process design record form used to record the most economical operational sequence for manufacturing or assembling a product is the
    A. flow process sheet
    B. standard process sheet
    C. job ticket
    D. routing sheet

_____ 8. The higher the quality of the item, the higher the
    A. volume
    B. availability
    C. rejection rate
    D. lot size numbers

(Continued on next page)

9-10. Short Answer.

9. Calculate the economical manufacturing lot size for manufacturing a steel rivet by cold heading under the following conditions:
   a. Number of parts that can be made per day 86,000
   b. Number of parts needed per day 50,000
   c. Total cost of setup in dollars $300
   d. Total cost of material, labor, and overhead per part, not including setup .... $.16
   e. Decimal fraction by which the cost of a part is increased if kept in storage one year .... .07

10. Calculate the economical manufacturing lot size for manufacturing an aluminum part on an automatic lathe under the following conditions:
   a. Number of parts that can be made per day 2880
   b. Number of parts needed per day 250
   c. Total cost of setup in dollars $450
   d. Total cost of material, labor, and overhead per part, not including setup .... $.35
   e. Decimal fraction by which the cost of a part is increased if kept in storage one year .... .07

Name _____

Score _____

UNIT 99
Product Marketing

1-5. Multiple Choice. Write the letter of the correct response to each statement or question in the space at the left.

_____   1. The function of industry that is concerned with sales and distribution of products is
    A. external relations   C. marketing
    B. finance and control   D. product planning

_____   2. Marketing research data is obtained by
    A. test marketing the product   C. researching company sales and ser-
    B. surveying present and potential cus-   vice records
       tomers   D. all of the above

_____   3. Developing sales forecasts for each product is the responsibility of those in charge of
    A. product planning   C. sales
    B. distribution   D. marketing research

_____   4. The marketing function that involves those activities needed to get the product to the customer is
    A. sales   C. product planning
    B. distribution   D. research

_____   5. Product servicing is a function of
    A. external relations   C. research and development
    B. marketing   D. all of the above

6-8. Short Answer. List three channels manufacturers use to distribute their products.

6. _____

7. _____

8. _____

9-10. Short Answer. Name two popular advertising media.

9. _____

10. _____

Name _____

Score _____

UNIT 100
Production Planning and Quality Control

1-7. Multiple Choice. Write the letter of the correct response to each statement or question in the space at the left.

_____ 1. Production planning is responsible for the functions of
   A. routing
   B. loading
   C. scheduling and dispatching
   D. all of the above

_____ 2. Calculating the time needed to process a job lot and charging it against available production time is known as
   A. loading
   B. scheduling
   C. routing
   D. dispatching

_____ 3. Authorizing the start of a manufacturing operation is known as
   A. scheduling
   B. loading
   C. dispatching
   D. initiating

_____ 4. An important production control form that provides a written record of the number of parts processed and the production time required is the
   A. standard process sheet
   B. flow process sheet
   C. schedule chart
   D. job ticket

_____ 5. An overall program of quality control is concerned with
   A. product design
   B. meeting design specifications
   C. product performance
   D. all of the above

_____ 6. Official inspectors are used to inspect
   A. purchased materials and parts
   B. work-in-process
   C. the finished product
   D. all of the above

_____ 7. Inspection of products that do not involve human safety is often done according to what plan?
   A. 100% inspection
   B. 50% inspection
   C. random inspection
   D. statistical sampling

8-9. Short Answer.

_____ 8. Which function determines the route the material must take through the plant?

_____ 9. Which department obtains the supplies and materials needed to make a product?

190

UNIT 101
Metalworking in the Manufacturing Laboratory

1-9. Multiple Choice. Write the letter of the correct response to each statement or question in the space at the left.

_____ 1. The first step in starting a classroom manufacturing activity is to
   A. determine the product to be manufactured
   B. form a company or corporation and elect or appoint company officers
   C. make a company organization chart
   D. write an organization manual

_____ 2. After the final design of the product has been approved, the next step is to
   A. make a prototype
   B. produce the standard process sheets
   C. design the production tooling needed
   D. make the production drawings

_____ 3. Standard process sheets should be made that give the correct operational sequence for
   A. making each product part
   B. assembling the product
   C. packaging the product
   D. all of the above

_____ 4. The sale price of the product should include
   A. all production costs
   B. all overhead costs
   C. a profit percentage
   D. all of the above

_____ 5. The number of products that must be sold before a profit can be made is called the
   A. profit point
   B. breakeven point
   C. economical manufacturing lot size
   D. none of the above

_____ 6. The route each part must take through a factory is planned by making a
   A. standard process sheet
   B. flow process sheet
   C. loading sheet
   D. job ticket

_____ 7. A short production run made to find and eliminate production problems before full scale production begins is called a
   A. run-through
   B. trouble-shooting run
   C. pilot production run
   D. operational sequence

_____ 8. Overhead costs include
   A. light and heat
   B. labor
   C. materials
   D. all of the above

_____ 9. Production costs include
   A. water and electricity
   B. labor
   C. marketing
   D. taxes